I
Elements: Music Theory, Songwriting, Lyrics & Creativity Explained

Copyright Notice

No part of this book may be reproduced or transmitted in any form whatsoever, electronic, or mechanical, including photocopying, recording, or by any information storage or retrieval system without expressed written, dated and signed permission from the author. All copyrights are reserved.

Disclaimer

Reasonable care has been taken to ensure that the information presented in this book is accurate. However, the reader should understand that the information provided does not constitute legal, medical or professional advice of any kind.

No Liability: this product is supplied "as is" and without warranties. All warranties, express or implied, are hereby disclaimed. Use of this product constitutes acceptance of the "No Liability" policy. If you do not agree with this policy, you are not permitted to use or distribute this product.

We shall not be liable for any losses or damages whatsoever (including, without limitation, consequential loss or damage) directly or indirectly arising from the use of this product.

Claim This Now

Music Business Skills for Musicians:

If you're in the music business, read on. Today you need to view yourself through the new rules of the music industry.

Those who play by them will succeed.

Gone are the old days where you would hope to get signed and then become a star (i.e., everything would be done for you).

Do you wonder why other artists are getting breaks and you are not?

MUSIC BUSINESS SKILLS FOR MUSICIANS

Make Money from Music, Discover The Music Industry and Explode Your Music Career!

TOMMY SWINDALI

Are You Ready To Start Earning REAL INCOME With Your Music?

https://www.subscribepage.com/musicbiz

Other Books by Tommy Swindali

In The Mix: Discover The Secrets to Becoming a Successful DJ

If you have ever dreamed of being a DJ with people dancing to your music and all whilst having the time of your life then this book will show you how. Find Out More

Music Production: Everything You Need To Know About Producing Music and Songwriting

Everything You Need To Know About Making Music In One Place! Grab your chance to own this comprehensive guide by Tommy Swindali. Covering everything you need to know about music production, as well as songwriting. Find Out More

Music Production: How to Produce Music, The Easy to Read Guide for Music Producers Introduction

You are about to discover proven steps and strategies from music producers on how to produce music, even if you have zero experience in recording and audio engineering. You will be able to learn everything you need to know in order to make your first single sound just the way you want it. Find Out More

Songwriting: Apply Proven Methods, Ideas and Exercises to Kickstart or Upgrade Your Songwriting

Have you ever listened to a song and thought "wow, if only I could write a song like that"? Well, you can now learn all the secrets on how to write beautiful music with this guide to songwriting! [Find Out More](#)

Table Of Contents

Introduction

Chapter 1. The Elusive Nature of Music

Why Write Music

How To Understand Music

Chapter 2. Music Theory Matters

Music Theory In Brief

Myths About Music Theory Debunked

The Importance Of Music Theory

Chapter 3. The Language Of Music: Basic Music Theory For Beginners

Music Notes

Scales

Scale Degree

Intervals

Chords, chord progressions, and chord extensions

Chapter 4. The Basics of Reading and Writing Music

Key Music Elements You Need To Know In Reading Music

The Basic Symbols Of Notation

Chapter 5. Music and Creativity

The Concept Of Creativity In Music

What You Need To Unleash Your Creativity

The Creative Process

Characteristics Of Creative Individuals

How To Unleash The Creativity In You

Chapter 6. The Essentials of Songwriting

Principles Of Art Applied In Songwriting

The Fundamental Aspects Of Songwriting

Chapter 7. Writing the Lyrics of the Song

Simplicity

Focus

Titles

First lines

Rhyme

Poetic Devices

Prosody and Meter

Chapter 8. The Pull of Song Hooks

What Is A Hook?

Characteristics Of Great Song Hooks

A Motif Is Not A Hook

Types Of Hooks

Guide to writing hooks

Chapter 9. What you Need to Know Before Writing Your Song

Where to start creating your song

Lyrics matter

Record your moment of inspiration when it comes.

Write from your experience

Don't be afraid to collaborate with other musicians

Keep your song simple and build on it.

Take breaks every now and then.

Don't overdo your thinking.

Welcome feedback.

Don't be afraid of failing.

Chapter 10. Write Your Song with These Easy-to follow-Steps

Start With The Title

Choose Your Song Structure

Bring Life To Your Song Through Images And Action Words

Look For The Melody In Your Lyrics

Chapter 11. Get into the Songwriting Business

How To Protect Your Songs

A Guide To Finding A Good Publisher

Publishing Your Songs

The Role Of The Publisher

Being Your Own Publisher

Guide To Starting Your Own Publishing Company

Conclusion

Introduction

"When you're at odds with yourself, it's hard to create. Sometimes the writing process is as easy as opening up the window and letting in the breeze. And sometimes it's like chiseling away at a block of granite with a pencil."

— Anthony Kiedis

Even the most successful songwriters recognize that music is a hard beast to tame. Sometimes, inspiration strikes in such a way that the melody and the beat just flows like spring water. And sometimes, it's like drawing blood from a rock.

This book is for anyone new to the craft. It's for those who want to build a good foundation for making music.

It's all about music and its elements. It explains everything you need to know to write songs.

The book starts with a discussion of the abstract and complex concept that is Music, and how one gets to know and understand what music is about.

Despite the complexity of music, there's always been something alluring about it.

The love of music is innate in many people. Many may not understand it, but its pull is such that we respond consciously or subconsciously. We tap our foot to the tune. We nod our head to the beat. We hum. Music is that pervading. Music is energy. It is emotion. It is expression. It is our hopes, dreams, loves, and fears all rolled into one in all their sonoric glory.

The things music represents are universal. But when songwriters try to capture the beauty of sounds by writing songs about their emotions – experienced or imagined -- many succeed, while others fail.

Some songwriters do get the inspiration to write songs. They start to write, only to get stuck somewhere in the process. While others may see this lull as a natural occurrence in a songwriting cycle, others get despondent and turn their back on songwriting altogether.

This is unfortunate especially for those who have a penchant for it but are just afraid of failure, or mistakenly believe that they just don't have the natural ability to do so.

Making music may seem difficult. But you'd be surprised to know that it is within your reach. Make no mistake, music and songwriting is complex. But it can be learned. Some part of you likely already knows a few things, and you'll realize how accessible it is when you break it down to its components.

If you are passionate about songs but find composing music and writing songs difficult, read on. The book comes with simple explanations of the materials you need to write songs, such as music elements, aspects of songwriting, and the basic signs and symbols you need to write music.

Music is life. If you have the passion and the reasons for wanting to write songs, hold on to it. Do it for yourself. At first it may seem like you're making music that no one but you hears, and that's fine. Create for creativity's sake. There's always beauty in bringing something to life

This book will help you find what you are missing and carry you on to success with songwriting.

Thanks for buying this book. I hope you enjoy it!

Chapter 1. The Elusive Nature of Music

Grasping the essence of music through our senses is not always easy.

It's rather elusive. Some things that give us pleasures are definite, but music is something we can't touch, and its very nature makes it rather ephemeral. Unlike with food, for example, where we can always look to the nutritional for guidance, there's no such thing with music. What you consider as music may sound like noise or nonsense to others.

But what we do know is that music – or at least certain types for certain people, is pleasurable.

There just seems to be something in music which moves us on a deeper level. It appears that we understand music, but knowing what music is and how it works is another thing.

One thing is certain, music is essential to us. You see the significant role of music throughout man's history.

That thing called music

Music is defined in many ways, depending on where you are coming from. An anthropologist's definition of music is different from that of a sociologist. A sociologist takes music in a cultural context. A Psychologist connects music to the well-being of a person.

For artists and musicians, music is an art form that is deeply embedded in human nature. Fundamentally, music is an ordered combination of sound in time, expressing ideas and emotions through the elements of melody, rhythm, texture, and harmony.

The process of knowing music

You don't have to be an expert in music to enjoy music. Knowing music does not entail limiting yourself within the boundaries of rules. Nor is it the kind of knowledge that makes you afraid of what happens when you go beyond the boundaries.

Unlike the other sciences, music occupies a different space which could be necessary to man's inner equilibrium. Music, in a way, responds to man's varying needs and fulfills different functions.

The act of knowing something, or anything for that matter, involves two phases:

Knowledge is acquired first on the *conscious* level – the rational and conscious world.

The second phase calls for assimilation, where what is learned enters the *unconscious* through constant practice.

Take the case of learning a language. You come across a new word (the consciousness), and you fix it in your mind through repetition and memorization. The second phase (the unconscious) is where you assimilate the new word by using it as often as the opportunity provides. When the word has been assimilated in the unconscious, it comes out spontaneously.

The same process is true in acquiring knowledge of music. The sound enters the conscious phase and is assimilated in the unconscious through constant exposure and practice. Once assimilated, music comes out spontaneously, without conscious deliberation.

For the composer or songwriter, music holds many surprises. Other knowledge opens up to the songwriter which are not learned but invented. And, with the knowledge acquired, the songwriter must then find one's voice and define one's personal identity.

But, the songwriter must first find, evaluate, and use what was learned before these can be assimilated. Further, what is assimilated is not the code of rules but the songwriter's expressive objectives. The experience produced by the songwriter that is beyond knowledge is emotional.

Knowledge which is based on emotion is how a songwriter communicates the musical ideas to listeners. The kind of knowing a composer or songwriter needs moves between the conscious and the unconscious levels. It is a constant back and forth movement that enriches both levels. This is also what's behind the elusive beauty of music.

Why Write Music

There are varied reasons why people write. The common belief is that these writers want a known artist to record their songs. That may be true to many artists, but there are many other reasons why people write.

The need to say something. Not all communication use words. Words may not be enough to express what one feels. Finding no words to convey their message to the world, they resort to songs. The message could be anything – from religious or moral, an experience like joy or grief, or the promotion of an idea or a cause.

The inspiration to write. You might have heard people say about waking up with a song in their head. Or have a tune crop up in mind and claiming not to know where it comes from. Inspiration could strike anytime, and there is this urge to write it down when it comes.

Writing a song is therapeutic. For a literary writer, it feels good to write on paper and let all the feeling out. The same is true for a songwriter. In the moment of writing songs, the thought of having your songs recorded by a major artist or to be heard by people is not the goal. You simply want to get all that stuff out of your chest.

Songwriters want to perform original songs. Some songwriters love performing, but not the cover songs. So, they write their songs and, in the process, define themselves as performers.

They want to hear their songs sung by others. These are the merchandise songs written by songwriters. They love to hear their songs performed by others and earn money at the same time. These types of people have to work differently. They need to imagine and speculate what the recording artist would say and become the voice of that artist.

It is the process of writing which is loved. These writers write for the love of writing. They don't do it for others, nor do they feel the need to let go of stuff out of their chests. They write songs for their satisfaction.

How To Understand Music

While you are on your journey to knowing and learning music, you cannot avoid listening to music as it is all around us. Rather than get sidetracked from your goal of listening, performing, or creating music, here are guides to make the most of your musical experience by understanding the music you hear.

Understanding the lyrics and enjoying the song

<u>Find the lyrics and follow along</u>. The first thing in understanding the lyrics is to really understand them. The lyrics and the melody support each other. The melody communicates the emotion; it is also the first thing that catches the attention of the listener. The lyrics tell the story. Melody and lyrics combine, add the conviction of the songwriter, completes the song.

So, get hold of the lyrics, follow along, and make sense of the song. Making sense of the song makes you understand what the song is about and why the title.

As an exercise, listen to Adele's <u>"Hello."</u> The song is about sadness and heartbreak. The title "Hello" tells you the writer is reaching out to people out there.

Some song titles may seem strange to you. A way to make sense of it is to look up references or words. Check out this instrumental music of Charles Mingus's <u>"Fables of Faubus."</u> If you searched Faubus and you will understand the choice of instrument and why the title; Orval Faubus was an Arkansas governor and a racist.

<u>Ask yourself how the lyrics and melody interact</u>.

Go through the lyrics as you listen to music. The instruments used in the music set the mood. It is how songwriters tell their stories. Music is abstract and subjective and can have different interpretations from listeners. So, if you were the writer, what music would you put to tell your story? Or, you can ask what moved the artist to choose a particular kind of music as a background.

Look up The Smiths' music and listen to it. They use happy and bouncy instruments that cloak melancholic, dark, and gloomy lyrics. It is suggestive of sadness beneath the surface of happy people. Or could it be the irony of life? What do you think?

<u>Stay alert for places where the artist emphasizes crucial lines</u>. Words are important, but how they are delivered is equally crucial. Watch for changes in the melody, occurrence of high notes, howls or moans, and for those pauses. Which phrases in the song stick in your memory and makes you sing them in your mind over and over? These phrases are the clues to the songs' importance.

A moan, a grunt, a howl, and hitting a high note all have meaning for the artist. Songs may appear like a love song until you reach a line which says otherwise (<u>Chelsea Hotel No. 2</u>).

<u>Search the net for the context of the song</u>. Songs are personal. Often, songs hide or hint at some personal experiences of writers. Knowing the context of the song makes you understand why the lyrics and why the music. If you fancy a song, take time to search the net and find out how the music came about. There may be something in the song you didn't know about, and that knowing enriches your experience of the song.

For example, listen to Eric Clapton's poignant song of *Tears in Heaven*. You'll have a strong emotional reaction when you learn the song is about Eric Clapton's son who died young.

<u>Listen for changes in tunes and when and where they occur</u>. Changing tunes is a technique used by advanced songwriters. Knowing the song turns can aid in understanding oblique or odd lyrics.

You get a turn when the lyrics make a sudden shift of direction, often confusing people. The shift, however, could be the message of the song. When you come across this kind of lyric, ask yourself these two important questions: How is the song's end line different from the beginning? How did the song get to the end?

For instance, _A simple twist of fate_ by Bob Dylan is written in the 3rd person in every verse. Until you reach the last verse and Dylan switch to the first person, using *I*. The song was an attempt to hide his emotions in someone else's story.

Participate in discussions or check out writings on music for greater appreciation. Join conversations or search online to find out what other people think about the lyrics. Joining conversations about music is a quick way of increasing understanding. It opens your mind to other possible interpretations of the song.

Have confidence in your own interpretation of the lyrics. Once a work of art is created and shared, you have the right to understand it in the way you interpret the work of art, just as much as everyone else. Remember that songs are personal. Therefore, no one can say what a song means for you, and because of this, your thoughts and opinion matter.

Finding appreciation for instrumentals
Listen to the music many times and make your own mood and impression. Jazz and classical music can be daunting to many people. Without the words to guide one, it is easy to feel strange and lost with the music. But, the truth is

they forget to tune in to their feelings when listening to instrumentals. So, if you come across jazz and classical music, ask yourself: Do you like the song or do you get bored with the music? How does the music flow from beginning to end?

<u>Closing your eyes when listening to instrumental music is a trick you can do.</u> Then visualize a scene in a movie that you think fits the music. Often, it helps to visualize music.

<u>Identify the basic structure of the music.</u> If you are listening to classical music, the structure could be a sonata, a binary, or a rondo. You can then identify your markers as references when you listen to it.

<u>Check the title.</u> The title is your first clue to understanding the music. It gives you the mood, the idea, and the image you can associate with the music.

If you are new to jazz and you want to listen to it, try Duke Elllington. The titles and the mood of his creations match. Just like his <u>"Sophisticated Lady"</u> and <u>"Take the A Train"</u>.

Or if you prefer classical music, try Beethoven's "<u>Moonlight Sonata</u>." It may sound dark, but it is perfect for a quiet and moonlit night.

<u>Listen to the individual instruments and gain an appreciation of the whole.</u> Instrumental music

communicates its story through a variety of instruments, providing a unique texture. Each instrument has a line to tell, yet the different instruments need to work together to come up with a unified storyline. Track each instrument throughout the music, and you'll be amazed at the nuances and the details you get.

Again, let us use Duke Ellington to illustrate this point. Listen to "Diminuendo and Crescendo in Blue" and discover how the different instruments balance each other and create complex melody lines.

Another way to appreciate music is to break it up into sections and see how each relate to other instruments. For instance, check what the strings are doing and how they balance with the horns.

Listen and see how the music flows from beginning to end. Listen to how the volume rises and falls and where these changes happen. What about the mood of the music? How and when does it shift from light and happy to somber and dark? How does the music or a section of it end? Does it end on a similar fashion (like a round) or in a different way? Music flows in time, which means it carries you on a ride. It holds your interest because you don't know what comes next or how it ends.

Understand dissonances and accept them. Dissonance can be hard on the uninitiated ears. They may sound off and weird, but this is not a mistake done by artists. Dissonances have a place in compositions, especially when the artist wishes to emphasize complex and negative emotions.

The thing to do when you encounter dissonances is to ask yourself what the role of the dissonance is to the story and why the composer would intentionally include a bad-sounding part in his music.

Check out Miles Davis' *Bitches Brew*. It is a combination of rock and jazz, mixed with African rhythms and influences. Davis, in this composition, attempts to show that music can no longer be contained in one genre. He explores this idea and pours it into *Bitches Brew*.

<u>Go deeper into specific genre and check out references</u>. Check out instrumental music and compare it from music that came before it. Often, music is a result of or because of what came before it. That is how music grows and gains power.

Take Jazz as an instance. Jazz may be complex and intimidating for some. But, jazz has evolved out of accessible music and in pace with American society. So, if you are interested in a type of music, search for earlier works and get insights into your preferred music.

<u>Learn an instrument or know music theory to enhance your understanding of music</u>. If your goal is only to listen

and talk about music, you can be confident with your ears, feelings, and mind. However, if your goal is to create music and not to be content with listening, it helps a great deal to know your music theory. You need not become a master, although understanding the process of creating music increases and adds depth to your understanding of music itself.

Chapter 2. Music Theory Matters

If you are a beginner in songwriting, you may have been told to learn music theory. Many music teachers insist on music theory as fundamental to music education. On the opposite side, there are also those who believe that having knowledge in music theory is no guarantee that you'll be a good performer and so, it's not necessary.

There may be people who can write music with minimal or no knowledge of music theory and their music is still enjoyable. Many may also enjoy listening to music without knowing what it is but would not know how, why, or what in music makes them enjoy it.

Music theory is what makes sense of music. If you are bent on writing songs, knowing the rules of the music language makes you more creative. You get to appreciate and enjoy your manipulation of music materials to achieve the idea and emotions you wish to convey.

Music Theory In Brief

Music Theory is the grammar of music which allows you to make sense of it. Learning the grammar of music, therefore, helps you understand what is going on in music when it flows in time.

In learning music theory, you encounter sets of rules. But, these rules are guidelines that describe:

- the music you hear

- explain the decisions songwriters and musicians make in the pieces

- help you achieve the effects you are after

- make you more creative by going beyond the boundaries of these rules, and

- play with the music materials you learned and will discover.

Music theory is challenging, but the skills you acquire from it is rewarding. You will learn concepts that will greatly help you in writing your songs, such as pitches, intervals, key signatures, time signatures, scales, scale degrees, chords, and chord progressions. These materials are your building blocks in constructing your melody, harmony, and rhythm.

Beyond the skills, knowing the language of music drives you to explore unexpected and interesting places with sound, and anticipate the expectations of your listeners.

Myths About Music Theory Debunked

Music theory stunts creativity. The idea that music theory stunts creativity is ludicrous. For instance, has your ability to read books suppressed your ability to communicate and be creative with words? It is possible this myth came from songwriters who found the need to defend their lack of theoretical knowledge.

Perfect Pitch is necessary to become a musician. One is said to have a perfect pitch if that person recognizes a pitch without reference to one other pitch. For instance, when you hear a person play a tone and you know it to be A# just because it sounds like it. This ability is rare and possessed by only a small percentage of musicians.

It is better to acquire the *relative pitch*, which is the ability to recognize a pitch in relation to another. With the relative pitch, you can be creative with the chord progression, imagine a melody, and know the relationship of instruments played in a band.

The "Mozart Effect" or listening to Mozart makes one more intelligent. This myth originated from a musical study published in Nature magazine in the 1990s. The study claims that people who listen to Mozart are likely to score high in spatial tasks. The result of this study was disproven in later studies. But, the public's fascination with the Mozart Effect remained.

The pop music of today is worse compared to other times in history. Whether myth or not, this would depend on how you define "worse." There may be truth to this myth. Take a look at the top charts of music in the 1960s and 1970s and compare it with today's top music. You cannot help but wonder what happened to music.

Times are different then and now. But the question remains: is today's music really worse? The answer depends on the kind of music exposure you experience. With the presence of the internet and so many platforms where musicians can showcase their stuff, you are likely to hear all kinds of music – both great and bad music.

Heavy Metal music cause negative effects to listeners, like self-harm and violence. Opinions on the effect of heavy metal music swings like a pendulum. A study made by Scheel and Westefeld on heavy metal music and adolescent suicidality claim that fans of heavy metal music had weak reasons for living and more thoughts of suicide. A later study on the impact of rock videos reported of having no effect on suicide rates.

The Importance Of Music Theory
Most of those who are uninitiated think of music theory as a set of rules to be followed. They are wrong or misguided. By not learning music theory, you miss making sense of what would otherwise be an anonymous sequence of notes or chords.

Whether you are a songwriter or an instrumentalist, there is much to gain by learning music theory, such as:

The ability to rapidly master a piece

If you know music theory, it speeds up your learning process. Think of music theory as a street map – you drive more efficiently if you know your way around an area. In music, it is easy to memorize a piece if you know where repetitions and landmarks are.

For example, the sonatas are long and structured pieces. The first movement of the sonata uses themes and variations. If you know your Sonata Form, you recognize the theme when it is repeated or when it is modified as a variation. Looking for the occurrence of the theme and its variation makes learning and performing a sonata fun. The same is true with songwriting.

Improvement of sight-reading ability

When you learn the structures of pieces and common chord progressions, you can predict the next measures. And, when you learn intervals, you can recognize their contours and larger patterns by sight, allowing you to read notes faster.

Heightened pleasure derived from music

With understanding comes greater appreciation. You will find this statement to be true to arts and crafts, or in anything that you do. So it is with music and songwriting.

When you are familiar with the features of a song or composition, your capacity for expression improves. And, you acquire relatability with the songs and the music played.

Improvise like a professional

Learning music theory enables you to predict logical chord progressions. With the ability to predict chord progressions, you can improvise music such that it sounds original, cohesive, and logical. Such ability also helps you during emergency performances when you find yourself off track, and you need to improvise without the audience noticing it.

Arrange simpler versions of musical pieces

If you know song construction and voice leading, you can arrange a simpler version of musical pieces. If you keep the voice lead intact, the song remains full and rich even with a simplified accompaniment.

Transcribe pieces by ear

When sheet music is not available, and you want to transcribe the music, your aural skills and knowledge in music theory will help you out. With music theory, you can transcribe by ear any piece you like for voice or instruments, and identify chords and key changes.

Helps you write music that sounds melodious and complete to listeners

While most materials in music theory are based on classical music, there are pieces, especially during the 18th and 19th centuries that serve as the foundation of music for all genres.

Whether you are a drummer, guitarist, or songwriter, knowledge of music theory will serve you well. The notation, chord progressions, and the concepts of rhythm and time are the same across genres and applicable to modern music.

And, some artists incorporated classical pieces into their songwriting. For example, <u>Galneryus *Angel of Salvation*</u> was inspired by "<u>Tchaikovsky's "Violin Concerto in D, Opus 35</u>."

Knowledge of music theory benefits different musicians. The last four items listed above are specific to songwriters.

Chapter 3. The Language Of Music: Basic Music Theory For Beginners

You may doubt the benefit you get out of learning music theory. But you better believe it that your level of understanding of music theory will make or break your dream of becoming a proficient musician – whether as a guitarist, song performer, or a songwriter.

Any profession has its own language comprising technical terms understood only by members of that line of work. A chemist has a mastery of the periodic table, the computer programmer is a master of binaries, and so with the other professions.

Music, too, has its own language. You will most certainly get lost in the maze of music jargon if you do not know its language. But, if you take the time to know music, it will be easy to collaborate with other musicians and gain from their knowledge in the process. And, knowing the language will make you more creative.

To help you learn music, we start with the basics of music theory.

Music Notes
Think of music theory as learning a new language. Music makes use of the musical alphabet to represent sounds. The sounds made are represented by notes, and each note

is represented by a letter. In music, there are only seven letters: A, B, C, D, E, F, and G.

When you play the notes and reach G, you start with A again but in a higher pitch. The next set of seven letters with higher sounds is referred to as an octave. As you continue to play the set (A to G) moving up, you move to higher octaves. Try playing the piano from the bottom end going on to the top.

There are seven letters to start with, but there are actually 12 notes in total. You may be wondering how we arrived from 7 to 12.

The seven letters are natural notes. The five additional notes are the accidentals – notes that fall between the natural notes. The accidentals are represented by flats (♭) and sharps (#). The natural sign (♮) returns the note to its original tone. A flat is a half-step lower in pitch than the note it corresponds to, and a sharp is a half-step higher in pitch.

Scales

Now that you know the notes, we move on and put the notes together to create a scale. The notes are your building blocks in creating a scale.

A scale is a collection of musical notes ordered by pitch, and can either be in ascending or descending order. The scales are often used by musicians as a means to practice instrument fingering or preparation for the flexibility of fingers.

But in music theory, scales are the framework used to determine what notes to be used in melodies and chords. Therefore, knowing the different kinds of scales and how they are constructed provides a solid basis for choosing notes and chords for a specific piece of music or song.

There are different kinds of scale, commonly used among them is the major scale. The other scales are the minor and pentatonic scales, both of which have different patterns and convey different moods and emotions.

The scale is constructed by arranging whole-steps and half-steps into a pattern.

A half-step, or semitone as it is also called, is the distance between one note and the note adjacent to it, either before or after the adjacent note. Example: From A to A# or from A down to A♭.

A whole step or tone consists of two half-steps. Example: A to B.

Major Scale

The major scale sounds positive and is used by a composer to depict joy, hope, happiness, and a party atmosphere.

To create a major scale, the following pattern is used: whole, whole, half, whole, whole, whole, half steps or W-W-H-W-W-W-H.

To illustrate the major scale, let us use the C major scale, which is the easiest major scale. Using a keyboard, you start with C and play all the succeeding white keys until you reach the next C up.

This is how the C major scale goes:

C D E F G A B C where C to D is a whole tone, D to E a whole, E to F is a half tone, F to G a whole, G to A a whole, A to B a whole, and B to next C up is a half tone (W-W-H-W-W-W-H).

You can start on any note, follow the pattern and you will have a major scale.

Minor Scale

The minor scale sounds negative and is used to convey melancholic, sad, angry, and dramatic moods. There are three minor scales in music, sounding minor-like, but each having a unique character.

The natural minor scale follows this pattern: Whole, Half, Whole, Whole, Half, Whole, Whole. You will also notice that this minor scale has no sharps or flats. On a keyboard, the natural minor scale is played all on the white keys.

The harmonic minor scale conveys a stronger feel than the natural minor scale. The raised seventh note causes the difference in sound. It is easy to change the natural minor scale to the harmonic scale by using the same pattern as the natural minor, but with the raised seventh note followed by a half tone. The pattern then becomes:

Whole, Half, Whole, Whole, Half, Whole and a half, Half

Starting on A, we have A to B (whole), B to C (Half), C to D (whole), D to E (Whole), E to F (Half), F to G# (whole and a half), G# to A (Half).

The melodic minor scale can be tricky as the notes going up the scale are different when going down the scale. It becomes easy if you remember that you only have to change the ascending natural minor scale. Going down the scale, the melodic and the natural minor scale are the same.

To construct a melodic minor scale, raise the 6th and the 7th notes by a half tone. Your pattern then becomes Whole, Half, Whole, Whole, Whole, Whole, Half. Note that the melodic minor is used going up the scale and the natural minor when going down the scale.

Scale Degree

There are seven notes in a scale corresponding to seven degrees. Each note in a scale is named after its function and is assigned a number to tell its position in the scale. The names and the numbers apply to both major and minor scales.

The names have the function to create and release tension and decide on chord progressions to indicate the resolution of tension. And, use of names and numbers makes it convenient to remember note location than remembering the individual notes.

1st note in the scale – tonic (the root note)
2nd note – supertonic
3rd note – median
4th note – subdominant
5th note – dominant
6th note – submediant
7th note – leading note

The 7th note is called the leading note because it leads to the resolution of the piece as it goes back to its tonic note.

Intervals

The interval is the distance between two pitches or notes. They are identified by names, numbers, and the quality of the intervals.

The number intervals refer to the number of letter names found within the interval. It can also refer to the position of the notes or names on the staff. In counting the number interval, you count the lines and spaces where the interval is positioned, including the notes forming the interval.

Let us use as an example the fifth interval C to G (also referred to as P5). The notes from C to G include C-D-E-F-G. On the staff, you see the notes occupying five consecutive lines and two spaces. You can start on any note, count the number of lines and spaces occupied, and you will have your interval.

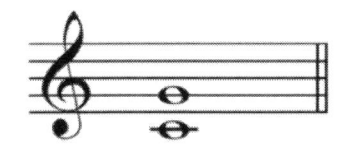

You can also identify your interval by counting the diatonic scale degrees, as you can see below.

Interval Name	Number of half steps
perfect unison (P1)	0
minor second (m2)	1
major second (M2)	2
minor third (m3)	3
major third (M3)	4
perfect fourth (P4)	5
augmented fourth (A4)	6
diminished fifth (d5)	6
perfect fifth (P5)	7
minor sixth (m6)	8
major sixth (M6)	9
minor seventh (m7)	10
major seventh (M7)	11
perfect octave (P8)	12

Intervals are either perfect or imperfect. The perfect intervals are the unison, the fourths and the fifths, and the octave. The imperfect intervals are seconds, thirds, sixths, and sevenths. The quality of an interval (in the perfect category) changes by using the diminished, augmented, and the perfect intervals. The quality of the imperfect intervals can also change by major, minor, and augmented intervals.

- A diminished interval is one-half step smaller than the perfect interval.
- An augmented interval is one-half step larger than the perfect interval.
- A minor interval is one-half step larger than the diminished
- A major is one-half step larger than the minor interval

- An augmented is one-half step larger than the major interval

Chords, chord progressions, and chord extensions

People who love and play music are, by nature, analytic. There may have been times when you attempted to analyze music recordings you want to learn, how the notes in the melody connect, what tempo to use, or how to move from bridge to chorus.

The chords and chord progressions are the answers to the mystery behind the music or song structure. They determine the character of the music and locate the connection between the music's logical and emotional sides.

Chord - A cord consists of 3 different notes. The use of "different" in the definition is important. Technically speaking, an octave does not count as a chord because of the repetition of the root note. Chords can be simple triads, complicated, or have extensions.

Triads - Triads are groups of three different notes. Triads have been the common harmonies found in Western music since the 16th century, both popular and classical. To figure out how and why chords work together, you need to know how they are constructed.

There are four basic types of triads identified through their structure.

1. Major triad - To build a major triad, start with any note; this is your root note. The second step is to add a note four half steps above the root. The last step is to add another note (above step 2) three half steps above. The second interval is a minor third. For instance, a C major triad consists of C, E, and G.

2. Minor triad – With the minor triad, you invert the intervals. The first interval above the root is a minor third (three half steps) and the second interval is a major third (four half steps). With C as root, your minor triad consists of C, E♭, and G.

   Note that whether your triad is a major or a minor, the top note above the root is always a perfect fifth. For the perfect fifth, you can count seven half-steps above the root. Therefore, in a triad, it is the middle pitch which determines if the triad is a major or a minor.

3. Diminished triad - In a diminished triad, all intervals used are minor intervals. In the example where C is the root, a diminished triad would be C, E♭, and G♭.

4. Augmented triad - In the augmented triad, all intervals used are major intervals. Where C is the root, the augmented interval would include C, E, and G#.

Chord Extensions - A chord extension is when you have a note that extends beyond the three-note triad and the octave. Another way of doing a chord extension is when you add a note to a chord which is beyond the 7th note of the scale. Still another way is to stack thirds above your triad.

The use of extended chord is fascinating as it creates a more harmonically complex and a richer sound than the regular major and minor triads. And, chord extensions can give you more interesting voice leading possibilities.

The chord extensions are the 7th, 9th, 11th, and 13th with the 13th as the farthest extension you can make.

Naming the chords - If you look at lead sheets, you might have observed labels like *C maj* or *CM*. These labels indicate a C major chord. With these representations, you may recognize the chord, but not the function. This is because the character and the purpose of the chord change with the key signature used.

For instance, the C major chord in a song that is in the key of C acts differently from a C major chord appearing in a song that is in the Key of F.

When analyzing chords, therefore, it is best to use Roman numerals. In this system, the Roman numerals used correspond to the scale degree of the root note.

Major triads use the upper case Roman numerals, while the minor triads use the lower case Roman numerals. A diminished triad uses the lowercase Roman numerals with a superscript circle beside it (°). An augmented triad uses the uppercase Roman numeral with a superscript plus sign beside it (+).

The different triads would appear like the figures below shown in the keys of C major and A minor:

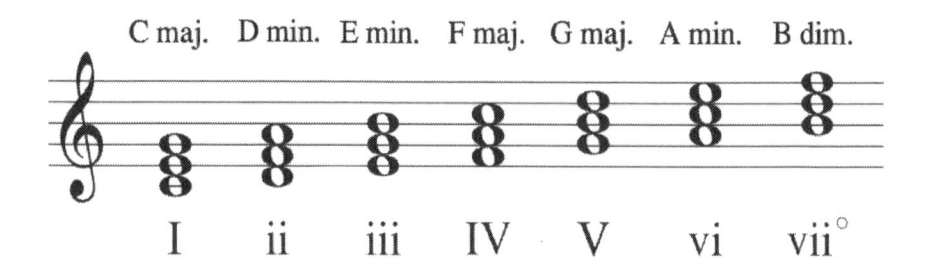

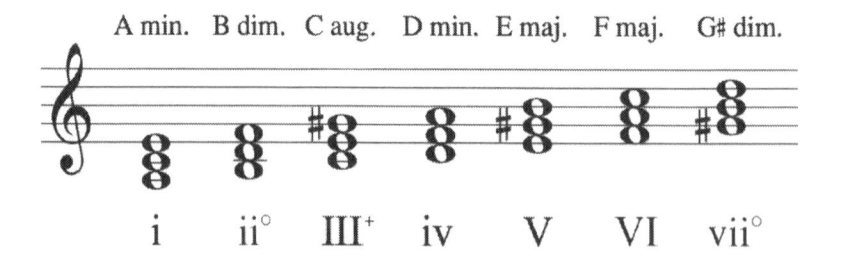

Chord Progression - Now you know how chords are built and how to recognize chords through its label. Let us move on and examine how they are used in songs with chord progressions.

A chord progression or harmonic progression, as it is also called, is an ordered series of chords. The chord progression is the foundation for creating the melody and harmony of your song and supports both rhythm and melody.

To show you how chords and chord progressions are used in a song, let us use Pachelbel's popular Canon in D major as an example.

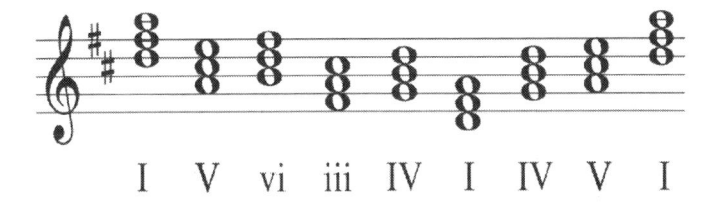

I   V   vi   iii   IV   I   IV   V   I

If you analyze the chord progression, you will see an introduction, a conflict, and a resolution, much like any good story. The progression starts with the I and V, which are considered the strong and stable chords, followed by the minor chords vi and iii. The minor chords sound weaker and, therefore, represent the conflict. The IV that follows represents the easing of tension and resolved by the appearance of the V, which then leads back to the root chord I.

Chapter 4. The Basics of Reading and Writing Music

Reading music is like entering a whole new world. For the uninitiated, the language used in music is strange, unknown, and has no sense at all. But for the musicians, it is a way to communicate musical ideas and emotional expressions.

It is not much different from the spoken language. The spoken language use letters and words to express ideas. Music use notes and symbols to communicate that which cannot be expressed by words. You will find sense in reading music if you think of the notes as the letters, the measures as the words, and the phrases as the sentences.

Key Music Elements You Need To Know In Reading Music

Pitch – This characteristic is one of the note's two vital aspects you should know to read music. In music, you will observe that some notes sound lower or higher than others. What makes the difference in sound is the pitch. You get to know the pitch through a series of letters.

Length of a note - Understanding this other important characteristic of the note allows you to read music. The length of the note refers to the duration of the sound or how long to hold a note. The appearance of the note indicates how long to hold the tone.

Speed and grouping of notes – The Italian words you see in a piece indicate how fast or how slow notes are performed.

Rhythm - Rhythm is what happens to the sound as it flows in time. It is about the movement and flow of sound and has a pattern which may either be simple (straight) or complex. Music's rhythm is also known as its pulse.

Volume - The volume is also known as the dynamics in music. What the volume is in a piece of music is indicated by Italian words.

Direction – There are signposts in music which tell you the direction the music flows. Here are some of the signposts or marks in a music sheet that tell the musicians where to go:

    a. - The tremolo sign that tells you the note is to be rapidly repeated.

    b. - The repeat sign which encloses musical passages, and is played more than once.

    c. - These are repeat marks that tell you to repeat the groups of beats or measures preceding the signs. The first sign with the single slash tells you to repeat the previous measure. The sign with the two slashes indicates the repetition of the previous two measures.

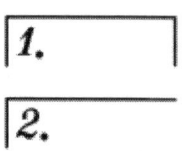

      d.   - These are your volta bracket signposts that tell you a repeated passage has a different ending on each different playing. Note that there may be more than two volta brackets in a piece of music.

      e. D.C. – In music, D.C. is the abbreviation for Da Capo. This mark instructs the performer to repeat the music from the beginning and stop until the word *Fine* is reached.

2. *Articulation* and *phrasing* are two elements which put expressions into different notes, bringing out the beauty in music.

      a. Phrasing – Phrasing can be lyrical or musical or both combined. In music, phrasing is a short passage often consisting of four measures and forms part of a larger unit.

To understand phrasing, listen to the Beatle's song "<u>Let it Be</u>." Let us analyze a verse in the song with the following lines:

When I find myself in times of trouble

Mother Mary comes to me

Speaking words of wisdom

Let it be

Line 1 in the song above is Phrase 1. As you can see, the line does not give a complete thought. Line 2 (Phrase 2) completes Phrase 1 and you now have a complete musical phrase. The same goes with Line 3 (Phrase 1) and Line 4 (Phrase 2). A complete musical phrase usually ends with a cadence which concludes the phrase.

b. Articulation – Articulation marks changes how the notes are played and establishes the relationship between them. Think of the articulation marks as forms of expressions which change, depending on the context they are used. These articulation marks are as follows:

i. Staccato – the note is played shorter than its value, usually half the value of the note. The dot is placed above the note if the stem is downward, and below the note if the stem is upward.

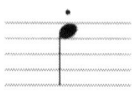

ii. Staccatissimo – The note is played even shorter than the staccato.

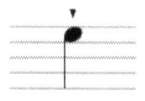

iii. Accent – The accent gives emphasis to a note. The note with the accent mark is played harder than the unaccented notes.

iv. Tenuto – The tenuto mark tells the performer to play the note at its full length of sound or longer.

v. Marcato – The marcato mark indicates the note is to be played more forcefully compared to a regular accented note.

vi. Fermata – With the fermata mark, a note, rest, or chord is held longer than its value.

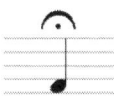

The Basic Symbols Of Notation

The fundamentals of music notations are the staff, the clefs, and the notes. To read music, you need to familiarize with these symbols.

Staff

A staff is a set of five lines and four spaces, with each line and space representing a letter, which in turn, represents a note. The lines and spaced are counted starting from the bottom.

The Staff

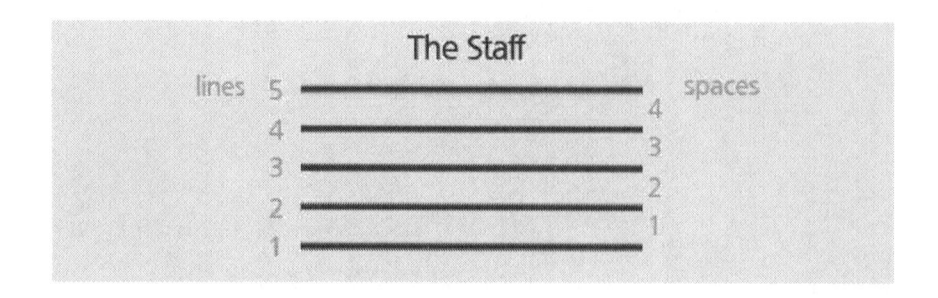

lines 5
4
3
2
1

spaces 4
3
2
1

Clef

The symbol of the musical clef tells the pitch of the note written on the staff. The clef sign is written on the left end of the staff. The most common clefs used are the treble or G clef and the bass or F clef.

The <u>treble clef or G clef</u>, so-called because the beginning of the symbol encircles the second line of the staff, tells that the line is G. The G clef is usually the first clef musicians learn in music theory.

The treble clef is represented by the symbol

𝄞

The treble clef indicates the notes on the staff, such as:

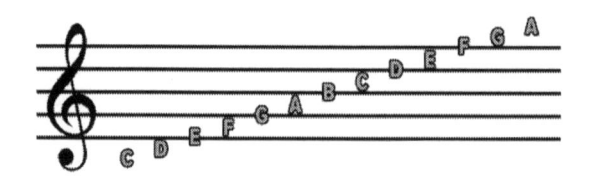

The bass or F-clef has this symbol:

𝄢

The F-clef derives its name from how it is positioned on the staff. Line F is between two dots of the F-clef symbol. The bass or F-clef indicates the low registers of music and is used for low-sounding instruments, such as the bass guitar, bassoon, double bass, cello, tuba, trombone, and timpani.

The alto clef is represented by this symbol:

𝄡

The alto clef got its name because its center, which is positioned at the middle of the staff, names the middle C. The alto clef is primarily used by the following instruments, the reason why many musicians do not know of this clef: alto trombone, viola, viola da gamba, and mandola.

The use of alto clef indicates the following notes found on the lines and spaces:

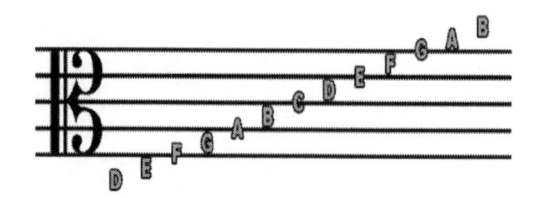

The tenor clef is represented by the same symbol as the alto clef, but with a different function. The center of the tenor clef is positioned on the fourth line starting from the bottom of the staff. The fourth line now represents the middle C.

When using the tenor clef, the lines and spaces have the following notes:

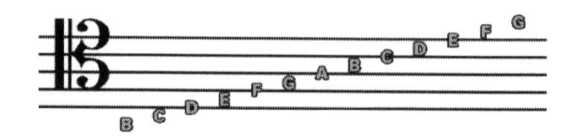

Note

A note indicates the pitch and duration of its sound; and, it also represents musical notation through its appearance.

A note consists of three parts: a head, stem, and the flag. The head is illustrated as filled (black) or open (white.) You can tell which note to perform from where the head sits on the staff – either on a space or a line.

When the head is found above or below the staff, you identify the note by a line drawn either through the head or above or below the head.

To illustrate how to perform the note heads through its position on the staff, check the notes B and C below:

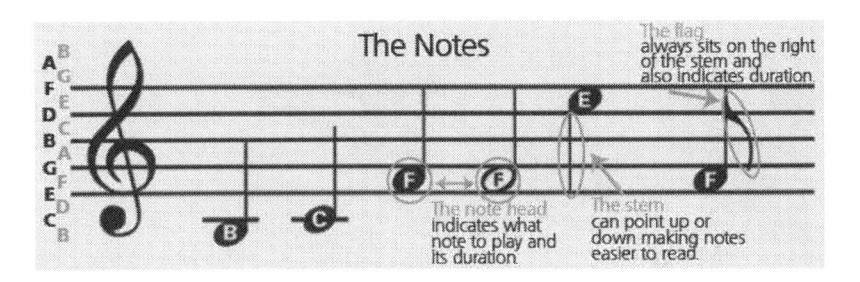

The note stem is the line you see attached to the head, pointing either up or down. The stem's direction is for the convenience of reading the note, and for neat placement on the staff; it attaches no other meaning to the note. As a general rule, the notes found at and above the B line have stems pointing downward, and those found at and below the B line have stems pointing upwards.

The note flag is the curvy mark you see attached at the end and to the right of the note stem. Its function is to indicate the length of the sound.

A single flag shortens the length or value of the note. Multiple flags shorten the note length even more.

Note Values

Where pitch is determined by the note's position on the staff, its appearance indicates duration.

A <u>Quarter note</u> has a black head with a stem and receives one beat. An open or white head is a <u>half note</u> and gets two beats. The white head without a stem and appears like an "o" is a whole note; it receives four beats.

An <u>eighth note</u> appears with a black head with a stem and a single flag. A <u>sixteenth note</u> will have two flags and a 32nd note three flags.

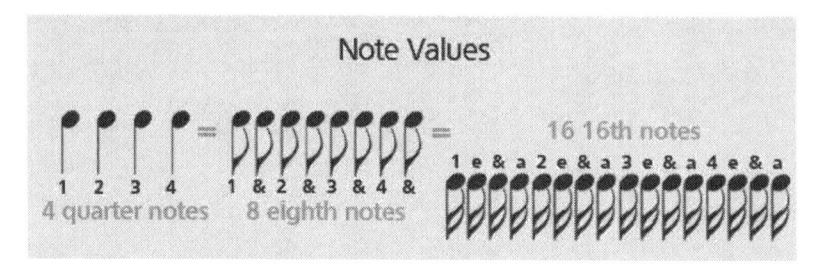

Note Values

4 quarter notes = 2 half notes = 1 whole note

Note Values

4 quarter notes = 8 eighth notes = 16 16th notes

You can extend the length of a note's duration by using dots placed after the note heads. A dot adds half the length of the note to which it is attached. For example, a dot after a half note is equal to the length of a half note and a quarter note.

The use of flags shortens the length of a note. The flag shortens the length of the note relative to the quarter note. Flags represent faster notes; you can also use beams that connect notes, like the notes shown below:

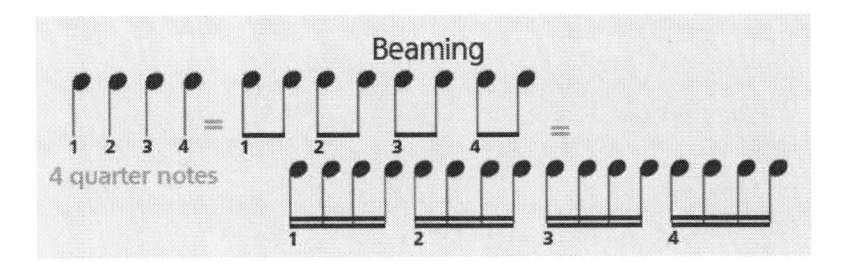

A flag is equivalent to half the value of a note. Therefore, one flag has one half the value of a quarter note, and a double flag means one-fourth of a quarter note.

When there is not a note to receive a beat, we use a rest which represents silence or no sound. A rest differs in appearance and has its equivalent in notes.

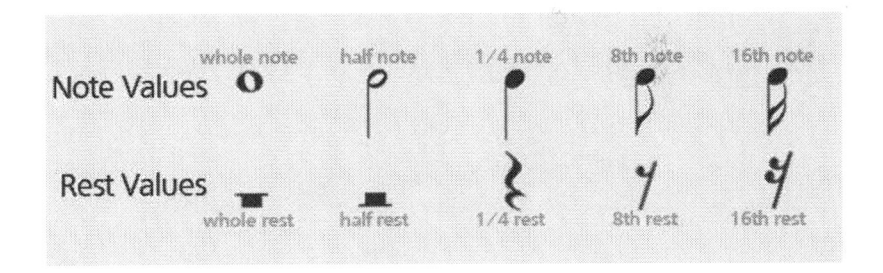

Time Signature

The time signature indicates the beat of the music. You may not be aware of it, but you respond to the beat of the music when you tap your foot, clap your hands or dance to the music heard.

The meter is represented by the time signature which appears like a fraction, having a top number and a bottom number. The top number indicates the number of pulse or beats in a measure. The bottom number indicates the note that receives one beat. The measure is a space on the staff with boundaries marked by vertical bar lines on each side.

To illustrate:

1) a 4/4 time signature means a measure contains four beats (indicated by the upper number), and that a quarter note has one beat (indicated by the lower number). Therefore, a measure should have four quarter notes.

2) A 3/4 time signature means a measure has three beats in it as indicated by the upper number. Each measure should have three quarter notes (indicated by the lower number), with each quarter note receiving one beat.

You may see a 4/4 time signature, but with two half notes in a measure instead of four quarter notes. The representation is right since a half note has two counts; therefore, two half notes would make four counts.

Tempo

The tempo represents the speed of the piece, or how fast or slow a piece is to be played. The tempo is indicated in two ways: a metric system found at the top of a piece of sheet music or by the use of Italian words.

For example, if you see at the top of the sheet music 60 BPM, which means beat per minute, it means you play a single note every second. To help musicians play at tempo when practicing, they use an instrument called the Metronome.

Examples of Italian words that indicate tempo are: Allegro, Largo, Presto, and Adagio.

Accidentals

In music, an accidental is a symbol that modifies the pitch of a note. An accidental raises the pitch of a note by a semitone with the use of the sharp (♯) or lower the pitch by a semitone through a flat (♭). The natural sign (♮) brings back the note's original pitch.

For example, placing a sharp beside C (C♯) raises the pitch of C a semitone higher. On a keyboard, you play C♯ on the black key on the right of C.

An example of a flat accidental is when a B has a flat sign beside it (B♭), it lowers the pitch by a semitone. On a keyboard, you play B♭ on the black key located on the left of B.

Key Signatures

A key signature is vital if you write or compose music. You may have heard a performer who asks an accompanist for the key before performing a song. Or a band member asking, "What key are we in?"

If you want to know the key of a song, count the number of sharps or flats found at the beginning of the sheet music and near the clef signs. The number of sharps or flats will tell you the key signature of a song. The location of the sharps or flats will also tell you which notes are affected by the signs.

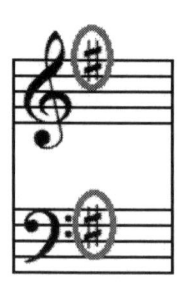

The sharps and flats in a key signature correspond to sharps and flats of the corresponding scale. The reference point of the key signature is always the scale's root note or tonic.

For easy learning, we give you these illustrations:

Key	Number of Sharps	Sharp Notes
C Major	0	
G Major	1	F#
D Major	2	F#, C#
A Major	3	F#, C#, G#
E Major	4	F#, C#, G#, D#
B Major	5	F#, C#, G#, D#, A#
F# Major	6	F#, C#, G#, D#, A#, E#
C# Major	7	F#, C#, G#, D#, A#, E#, B#

Key	Number of Flats	Flat Notes
C Major	0	
F Major	1	Bb
Bb Major	2	Bb, Eb
Eb Major	3	Bb, Eb, Ab
Ab Major	4	Bb, Eb, Ab, Db
Db Major	5	Bb, Eb, Ab, Db, Gb
Gb Major	6	Bb, Eb, Ab, Db, Gb, Cb
Cb Major	7	Bb, Eb, Ab, Db, Gb, Cb, Fb

In the diagrams below, observe the key signatures' placement and the position of the sharps and flats.

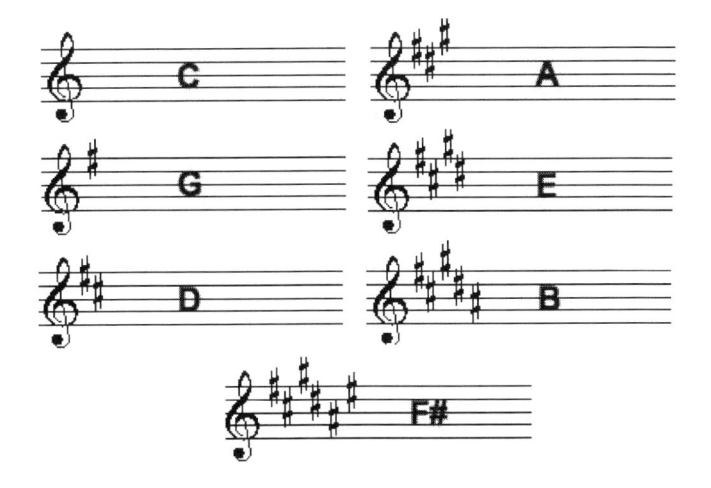

You can build your key signatures following the scale patterns you learned under the *scale* above.

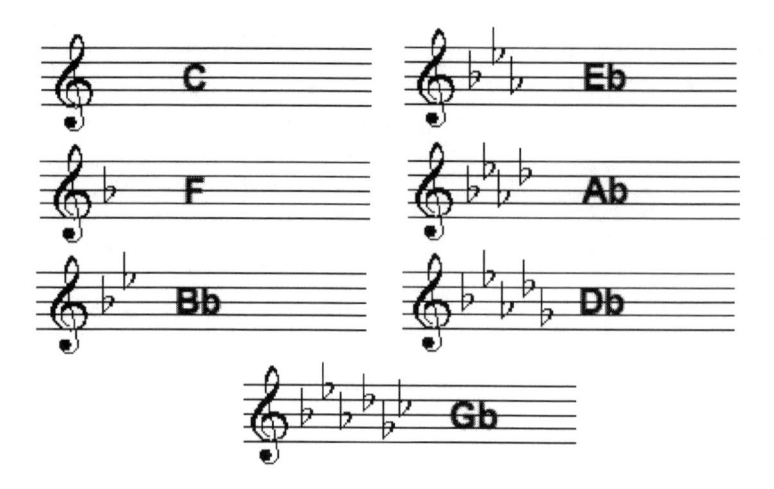

Chapter 5. Music and Creativity

Creativity is a concept that is hard to grasp and understand. Most people often attribute creativity to the arts and the artists as creative. Contrary to this belief, anyone can be creative. The concept, though, requires some measure of individual activity and behavior for one to be creative.

There is also the thought that the use of the term "creativity" is much abused. Like, when a mother refers to her child as creative for being able to read music. Or when a father says her 5-year old daughter is creative for she can draw a perfect quarter note.

Let's take a look at what creativity is and its place in music.

The Concept Of Creativity In Music
Creativity, in essence, is the capacity to generate new ideas that are appropriate and effective. Some people say that the original ideas generated are not all useful. Still, others say that creativity is at the core of humanity.

But more than the ideas themselves, creativity is about how we develop, understand, and communicate these ideas.

Creativity in music is having your mind engaged in an active and structured process of thinking in sound to come up with something new. Creative thinking is a dynamic thought process that moves alternately between thought/imagination and analysis and evaluation.

The movement from thought and imagination to analysis and evaluation involves skills and knowledge learned. However, creativity also requires enabling conditions that one gets outside of formal education. The enabling conditions and skills support each other to achieve what an artist or a songwriter is after.

What You Need To Unleash Your Creativity

Experts observed the activities of artists and categorized these activities into six components:

1. *Specific knowledge-based, expert knowledge.* This component relates to your knowledge of a specific topic about which you wish to be creative. Or, if you want to be creative in a specific topic, you need to acquire and develop sufficient knowledge about the subject.

    What is more, your knowledge should be sufficiently comprehensive such that you can connect ideas in a new way. This component requires high-level commitment and persistence on a topic.

In addition to being focused on a topic, you need to be open. For instance, you may have interpreted music at a particular time. Be open to other viable interpretations. And, you need to believe your interpretation at the moment is not set in concrete and absolute terms.

2. *Divergent thinking.* This component refers to how the artist thinks creatively about ideas. This includes how an individual:

   a. Explore and plan new paths

   b. Maintain and hold options for as long as you can

   c. Suspend judgment

   d. Fluency and flexibility

   e. Originality and relevance

   f. Re-structure and link ideas in different ways

   g. Elaborate or how well you can infer ideas to others

The idea of being creative is to be sensitive to problems or the ability to see and find problems. This trait, that is, the ability to detect problems, is the first step towards creative thinking.

People differ in how they see problems. Imagine the children who ask questions naturally. These questions are verbal expressions linked to the child's natural curiosity. It is a form of drive for knowledge and exploration. The same kind of characteristic you need to be sensitive to problems – a natural curiosity that drives you to explore and know.

Divergent thinking connects to different emotional aspects. A person is always susceptible to social and peer pressures. Due to emotional responses to these pressures, you get distracted and unable to see problems and ideas for your creation.

Divergent thinking requires a level of independence where you resist and don't get carried by group pressure.

3. *General Knowledge and Thinking.* To be able to think creatively and come up with a useful product, you need to:

- Have a broad perception and quick processing of ideas and perception
- store knowledge in a flexible memory
- analyze and synthesize ideas and knowledge
- reason and think logically

- be critical and evaluative

For creative thinking to happen, there needs to be a dynamic balance of the two components of divergent thinking and general knowledge.

4. *Motives and Motivation.* To produce creative results, you would need motives, task motivation, and drives, especially those that come from within you (intrinsic). These traits come out when you engage with new aspects of the task.

It is easy for these drives to come out if your environment is conducive and supportive of your creative efforts. For instance, children are naturally curious, feel a need for anything new, and a drive to explore and know. Parents or the learning environment often stunt these characteristics.

The same is true with creative adults. Their creativity is stunted by unsupportive people who give negative feedback. Or it could be that the environment you are in is full of distractions. You need a place where you can focus on novel ideas.

5. *Focus and commitment.* For creativity to flourish, you need perseverance, persistence, and commitment to the task at hand.

6. *Openness and Tolerance.* To be creative, you need to be open and able to tolerate ambiguities. This component characteristic refers to the ability to resist peer or group pressure, to maintain a nonconformist behavior, and to have an independent thinking. Ideas need not be right just because the majority in the group support them. Have confidence in your own ideas.

   Risks will always be present in anything that you do. But, risks should not deter you from being creative, making remote associations, being playful, and not be afraid to experiment and explore ideas.

The Creative Process

Creativity involves a complex process. A creative person goes through several phases in the process of creating. The creative process does not follow an orderly step or a definite order. Also, the process could either be of long or short duration.

Do not be surprised if you go through the process several times before you reach the desired outcome. Geniuses are known to have reworked their creations before finally getting satisfied with their work.

1. *Inspiration.* Inspiration is also referred to as the motive behind the creative process. It is the idea-

generating phase. There is no limit to the idea you can generate in this phase; it comes out spontaneously. You select from the ideas generated, experiment, and take risks.

Generating ideas is like mining for precious stones. You discard much of what you dig, but it doesn't stop you from digging. Nor would you look at the effort as a waste of time.

If you are having difficulty with this phase, ask yourself why. It could be that you are too critical of yourself. Or, you expect that generating ideas is easy and quick.

You might think that it is easy to generate musical ideas. Searching for ideas, however, includes finding your voice, reaching for emotions deep within yourself, and looking for a strong identification with the topic.

The inspiration phase is not the time to worry about musical structure, practicality, or the quality of the idea. Expect to reject 90% of your ideas, and you will not feel frustrated and discouraged. Free yourself and take risks.

<u>Mind set</u>. Generating ideas requires the right mindset. The right mindset means being focused, fearless, and free to explore ideas. And, it also requires you to be

spontaneous, joyful, risk-taker, intuitive, and improvisational.

Would-be songwriters often commit the common mistakes of being fearful and self-conscious. They often use inappropriate logical thinking that leads to weak and unoriginal ideas. And, budding songwriters have the tendency to accept the first idea that comes to mind, not bothering to explore other ideas.

2. *Clarification*. In this phase, you concentrate on your goals. To help you clarify your goal, ask yourself these questions:

    - What are you trying to accomplish?
    - What specific problem are you trying to solve?
    - What do you want to say?
    - How would you like the finished work to appear or sound?
    - How can I exploit the idea or ideas?
    - Where will this idea take me and what can I make out of it?

What you are trying to do in this phase is to clarify your objective -- the purpose of your work. If you don't focus, you lose direction and get distracted by the difficulties encountered in creating your work. When distraction happens, disengage yourself from the work and the obstacles and reflect on what you are trying to do.

When stuck in the process of creating, don't think of several alternatives. Instead, clarify where you want to go and how to get there. You might be surprised to see that the direction was obvious, but you were blinded and overwhelmed by the alternatives.

Clarifying your goal helps you get where you want to go.

<u>Mind Set</u>:. Clarifying your goal needs a strategic mindset, slow and unhurried but moving forward. You should be logical, analytical, and clear minded. Do not be afraid to ask difficult questions or seek help from another. Often, the reason a songwriter fails is not being able to clarify the problem.

3. *Distillation*. Distillation is the phase where you go over the ideas generated and identify which ones to develop. In this phase, you sift the ideas generated in the inspiration phase and evaluate these ideas based on your findings from the clarification phase. Once you have chosen the best ideas, you can start developing the ideas or combine them to come up with better ideas.

This phase is where your activity becomes self-critical. Here, you do an objective analysis and judgment, not a blind and dazzled spontaneity.

But, do not be overly critical of the work or you inhibit productivity altogether. Note that the ideas you work on are ideas, not solutions. Therefore, do not expect much from them. What matters is where these ideas take you, not the ideas themselves.

Mind Set: The mindset required of you in this phase is being positive, strategic, and dauntless. You have to be judgmental but optimistic of the ideas' direction, and courageous to take on original ideas. You will have to be realistic but open to possibilities.

A common mistake of songwriters is using familiar ideas or ideas used several times.

4. *Hard work*. When you work hard in a determined fashion on your ideas, you get to where you want to go. This phase is where the real work is done. Note, however, that hard work on your ideas involves the three phases of inspiration, distillation, and clarification.

Mind Set: Hard work requires persistent and positive about your work. You have to be deeply engaged and committed to your work. When after evaluating your work, you realize you have to repeat a cycle, be ready to respond to the results of your evaluation, and work positively on any observed shortcomings.

Hard work often discourages most songwriters or any artist, for that matter. They fail to make the best out of hard work. They become self-critical; and, uncertainty sets in. They interpret the weaknesses as lack of talent instead of the necessity to work harder or to use a different approach.

5. *Evaluation.* This phase is where you review your work in progress. Evaluate your work for strengths and weakness, and consider ways on how to improve your work. By evaluating, you eliminate the weaknesses you find and maximize strengths.

You might realize that you need to work hard to respond to positive suggestions for improvement. The working hard and evaluation phases often alternate, forming a new cycle. It will be easy for you if you understand that nothing gets perfect the first time. You may have to do the cycle several times to get to near perfection.

The repetitive nature of evaluation is the reason many would-be artists dislike it. It might interest you to know that creative people are inveterate revisors. But, when you look deep into the evaluation phase, this could be challenging and rewarding. If you have the musical passion, evaluation can get you fully absorbed in work. Besides, no work worth of merit can be produced without evaluation.

<u>Mind Set</u>: The evaluation phase requires you to be self-critical but confident of your vision. The mindset requires belief in your ability to create and develop ideas; to go where ideas take you. Further, be willing to learn from the mistakes made in the process of creation; view the mistakes as opportunities for improvement.

Those songwriters who see criticisms as threats and personalize negative feedback fail on their efforts to create something valuable.

6. *Incubation.* The incubation phase is where you distance yourself from work and leave it alone for a while, without stopping to think about it occasionally.

If you stop working on a project for some time or work on other things, you allow your subconscious time to pay attention to other problems encountered. And, taking time off from your project allows you to evaluate your ideas better.

Incubation is a tremendous help during the inspiration and hard work phases. It is how great artists get their creations done. Successful artists take time out for the incubation phase and not worry over sketchy ideas, inconsistencies, and loose ends. They patiently wait until something turns up.

<u>Mind Set</u>: Take a break from a project and allow your subconscious to work in a slow and unhurried pace. Expect to encounter difficulties, but trust yourself to find your way around them. Do not panic, as this will cause you to choose a weak solution.

Note that each phase in the process of creativity requires a different mindset. It is possible for you to switch, time and again, between different mindsets to accomplish your task. To use an inappropriate mindset can be disastrous to your creativity.

For instance, being overly critical and not careful with the ideas will hinder you from generating original ideas. On the other hand, you cannot clarify your goal if you are not critical of your work and objectives.

Most artists respond to the phases in different ways. Some are stronger in some phases, while others struggle with it. The differences in responses can be attributed to people's different mindsets.

Our mindset depends on our personalities. But, we can dig deep within us and learn how to use the right mindset.

A mindset is a belief that tells us how to handle situations, how we sort out things and ideas, and what we should do. But, a mindset is not just a belief. It is an internal framework directing us to what we deem is important, so we don't get overwhelmed with information. A mindset suggests sensible goals, so we know what to achieve.

If you believe that you do not possess the appropriate mindset for a specific phase in the process of creativity, take heart for you can change your mindset. A mindset is something in our minds, and the good news is, we can change our minds.

Characteristics Of Creative Individuals

Creative individuals are difficult to describe since traits vary according to time and context. For instance, the Renaissance artists differ from post-Renaissance artists. Artists from later Renaissance were described as mad and savage, while early Renaissance artists were considered sensible and tame. Abstract expressionism artists were described as brooding, sullen, and antisocial. But mentors describe these artists as very creative.

Creative individuals show complex personalities, manifesting <u>contradictory extremes</u>. They tend to show a wide range of human possibilities. These qualities are also present in all of us. However, most people are trained to develop only an aspect, like emphasizing competitiveness and dislike cooperation and collaboration. A creative person, however, can be both cooperative and aggressive at the same time or at different times.

Though a creative person moves from one extreme behavior to another, it does not mean having a wishy-washy personality. The move from one extreme to the other is conditioned by the occasion. It is, therefore, by intention or choice.

Creative persons are familiar with both extremes, moving from one to the other with equal intensity and without inner conflict. These extremes in artists manifest in the following:

1. Show enormous energy, but can also be at rest and quiet
2. Tend to be smart, yet naïve at the same time
3. Can be playful yet disciplined or responsible and irresponsible
4. Alternates without effort between imagination and fantasy on one end and reality at the other
5. Has opposite tendencies towards introversion and extroversion

6. They are remarkably humble, but proud at the same time

7. They dislike strict gender role stereotyping but tends toward androgyny

8. Most often, creative people are described as rebellious and independent

9. They are passionate about their creation but can be objective about it.

10. Creative individuals are open and sensitive, exposing themselves to pain and suffering. But, they are capable of experiencing much enjoyment.

How To Unleash The Creativity In You

Creativity in music is viewed as the human capacity for problem-solving, inventing, and exploring imaginative worlds. For the imagined world to be believable, it has to be logical and consistent. Working on the imagined word requires the problem-solving ability. A songwriter needs to solve how to combine music elements to make it work.

But, many talents go to waste or are diminished. Obstacles exist that prevent promising songwriters from pursuing their dreams. There are negative attitudes that stand in the way of developing talents, such as:

- Minimizing the value of art. To be a songwriter is difficult and often does not "pay off." Any person who wants to be an artist, including one who wishes to become a songwriter, needs a minimum of support for the ambition and should be respected.

- The private club attitude. This attitude is a common obstacle met by beginning songwriters. The belief is that composers belong to an exclusive club, and acceptance is determined through a small elite. The idea is exclusion based on judgment and taste of supposed arbiters. Though studies have proven this wrong, the belief- ungenerous and closed though it is - remains.

- Artificial limits. Another obstacle which limits and excludes budding songwriters are criteria which include age, sex, race, or style. Let us pick on style as an artificial limit. Style is fundamentally the expression of a person's personality, not a trend. Style tends to emerge in an individual naturally over time. One does not choose style intellectually.

- The modernity mania. If you check history, you will see that many great composers were considered conservative in their own time, like Brahms and Bach. Judgment on modernity is shallow, and what is modern today may not be modern tomorrow.

- Confusion between arrogance and ambition. A songwriter must be confident in the craft to create songs. Having confidence is an honest ambition and should not be confused with ego-driven plans for popularity. When a budding songwriter gets mocked for creative ambition, the legitimacy of the ambition is undermined, leading to the artist's incapability to produce songs.

- Disrespect for craftsmanship. Composition is craftsmanship first – which is the refined use of ideas and musical materials - before it becomes an art. Judging the songs as art without first seeing it as a craft is unreliable. Judgment then becomes arbitrary and results to discouraging hard work.

- Over-intellectualizing. Creativity is in the totality of the person, not just the intellect. Over insistence on the intellect and trying to dissect everything analytically is dangerous for the budding songwriter. The songwriter may not even be aware of the sources of inspiration.

Now that you know of obstacles to your creativity that you are likely to encounter, you can set them aside and focus on how to unleash your creativity.

Here are a few tips:

1. Have a notebook handy. You never know when an idea crops up. It is easier to write them down for memory recall if you have a notepad with you wherever you go. You can write your lines shorter or longer or simply write the main lines.

2. Develop techniques in writing small parts. It is easier to work on one section than work on all sections in one sitting.

3. Have an extra-musical stimulation. Stop stressing and try to remember what in songwriting you enjoy most.

4. See live music. Seeing live music can be a source of inspiration to see performers perform.

5. Look for creativity outside of music. Try to see other art forms. Some songwriters write based on movies they saw or books they have read. Often, exposure to other art forms can be a source of idea for your song.

6. Create something out of nothing. Listen to Beatle's song "I am Only Sleeping" and see how it is possible to create a song even when bored, half asleep or tired.

7. Get a change of environment. For instance, if you find yourself alone most of the time, surround yourself with friends or musicians. If you are in the city, explore the country. If you favor classical music, try to listen to pop music.

Chapter 6. The Essentials of Songwriting

Anybody can be creative; it is innate in man to want to create. This ability is within us and just waiting to be tapped, shaped, honed, and used. Which means is you can be a songwriter.

But, it is not only a matter of writing songs. You would also want to do it well to succeed in your endeavor. There are a great number of songwriters out there, but many fail to achieve what they are after. They get stuck on the amateur level.

Amateur songwriters view the craft of writing songs in a single-dimensional work. They see songwriting as a single process and with the sole purpose of selling their songs to a professional singer. They fail to see that writing songs is a multi-dimensional world that involves many areas.

Principles Of Art Applied In Songwriting
Music is an art form, and therefore has the same basic principles as others. In learning how to write songs, you will encounter the principles of art applied to the making of your songs. It is, therefore, a big help for you to know

what these principles are and how they convey your intent to your listeners.

Contrast

This principle refers to the difference between the elements in music. Using contrast makes each element stronger than the others. When these elements are placed near each other, a part in the composition becomes dominant and emphasized; the contrast then catches the listener's attention.

For instance, a loud musical line followed by a soft line is an example of contrast and emphasis. The loud and soft in music is referred to as dynamics, and its use in songs produces an impact on the listeners. An example of contrast in dynamics is Beau's "Silence Returns". The song shows dynamic contrast with Beau singing about silence, which became un-silent with the entry of instruments.

And, you can also create rhythmic, melodic, and harmonic contrasts in songs.

Balance

This refers to the weight of the elements of a composition. It is a sense of feeling that the work is stable and feels "right." An imbalance leads to a feeling of discomfort to the viewer or listener.

In music, a balance exists through the level of two or more voices, instruments, or sounds playing. An imbalance exists where the instruments overpower the voice or where the instruments play with equal volume. You can also have balance in tonal quality, and not just on volume.

Movement

In the visual arts, a sense of movement is achieved by using the elements of art, such that the viewers' eyes are guided within and around the image.

In music, the movement provides a sense of progress or a sense of momentum within a piece that keeps listeners from getting bored. Usually, as the song progresses, the intensity and energy of the song build up.

You can build intensity in your song by changing the energy according to:

- tone and pitch
- rapid note changes
- level of ornamentation
- use of a broad harmonic content.

Pattern

Pattern refers to the repetition of any element in art, for instance, the repetition of lines and shapes. In music, pattern refers to the repetition of sequences or sound. The pattern is also referred to as the restatement, like the restatement of a theme.

It is innate in us to recognize and make sense of patterns. A songwriter can take advantage of pattern recognition to draw the listeners to the song's patterns.

Songwriters often value the importance of patterns in chord progressions, rhythms, and lyrics. It is the melodic pattern that is often neglected. There are two ways that repetition can make your melody attractive: the melodic hook and the melodic motif.

Unity and Variety

Unity in art creates a sense of wholeness. By putting together similar elements in such a way that they seem to harmonize, there is unity in an artwork. Variety is what adds interest to the artwork by using contrasting elements in the composition.

In music, unity is the use of repetition or similar ideas in a song. Variety is introducing something new, adding novel ideas, elements or new patterns to a song.

A songwriter, however, needs to balance the principles of unity and variety in a song. You achieve a solid balance when your listeners pay attention to your song for long.

The Fundamental Aspects Of Songwriting

Some people listen to the music's structure and not to the pleasing sound. The analytic listeners may be acceptable to some musicians, but not to those who aspire to be successful songwriters. For songwriters, the beauty of the creation is in the sound.

While the structure of music gives form to it, it is the mix of components that produces the sonic beauty that people appreciate.

Form

The form in songs consists of verses, a chorus, and occasionally, a bridge. A verse is where the harmony and melody repeats, but the lyric changes. A chorus repeats lyrically and musically, and the bridge appears once, either in its music or the lyrics.

For convenience, the verse, chorus, and bridge sections are referred to by capital letters A (verse), B (chorus), and C (bridge.) Using these sections, you can build your idea or storyline, convey your point on the chorus or the bridge, and lead your song to a satisfying conclusion.

It has become fashionable today to have a pre-chorus or a climb. The pre-chorus is a different section with two rhymed lines that pulls the verse and ascends towards the chorus. It produces the effect of increasing the tension through a delay in the appearance of the chorus.

The form of your song is the sections put together. When you create your song, what you are actually doing is telling your listeners what you want to say (verses), saying it (chorus or the bridge) and telling them what you said (the conclusion.)

A closer look at the parts of a song

a. Verse

This section is your primary means of conveying the message of your song. Another of its function is to "set up" or lead to – musically and lyrically – the chorus, another verse, the bridge, the title or the hook. If your song has none of these functions, then your song is not working.

Take not of these characteristics of verses:

- The lyric is different from verse to verse. It may contain new information for each verse or information from previous verses, like the title line if your song has no chorus.

- Each verse has the same melody. You can be flexible with your melodic line and have slight variations to make way for the lyric. The purpose of repeating the melodic line is to make it easy for the listeners to focus on the changing lyric.

b. Chorus

In current songwriting fashion, the chorus (also referred to as the refrain) places the emotion, essence, and song meaning into a statement that is simple and easy to remember. Listen to "I Can Love You Like That" which exemplifies the role of the chorus.

The chorus is the section of the song which is also referred to as the *hook,* so-called as it is the most memorable line or lines in the song, and aims to catch the attention of the listener. And, the chorus makes a broader statement with more repetitions than the verse.

Chorus characteristics:

- The melody is the same for each verse
- You see the title of the song in the first or last line, maybe more
- The lyric is the same for each repeated chorus. It is possible, though, to have new information in a repeated chorus to develop your story. An example of this last characteristic is the *turnaround,* a term

and a tactic most often found in country music. New information or the twist is entered in the last chorus.

Listen to the chorus line of "I Wanna Be There". Notice that in the chorus, the title is found in the starting lines of 1, 2, 4, 5, and 8. The effect of the repetition is that the listeners learn the song, and can easily sing along with the tune. The writer can change information in the chorus and not worry about the listener losing the listeners' interest.

c. Bridge

You might have heard the bridge referred to as *release*. The bridge occupies an important place in a song. It is usually found two-thirds into the song when listeners start to get bored with the constant melodic repetition. With the bridge, you bring your listeners back to attention.

You can use any device to break the boredom factor, such as:

- The principle of contrasts
- Use of instrumentals
- A change in the melodic line

- Lyrically, you can repeat the idea of the song in a different or new way, like changing from *You* to *I*

Bridge characteristics:

- The melody differs from the chorus or the verse. Occasionally, though, part of the melodic line in the verse or chorus can be used in the bridge.
- Though not a rule, the title or the hook is not contained in the bridge. The decision to use the title in the bridge depends on the songwriter's preference and the number of repetitions where the title appears.
- The bridge usually occurs once, though it can be repeated as an extension of the verse or chorus.
- It is seldom more than eight bars long. Note that a bridge is only a diversion or a break, and not the song itself.
- The inclusion of the bridge is optional.

d. Pre-chorus

This section of a song is gaining popularity in contemporary music and found in pop, hip-hop, R&B, and lately, the country music. You may have come across the other names which refer to pre-chorus: lift, set-up, climb, B-hook, pre-hook, and channel.

The pre-chorus is different from the bridge, the verse and the chorus. Its function is to increase the level of interest of the listeners, making the song exciting.

Characteristics Of Pre-Choruses:

- They come before the chorus

- They come before *each* chorus, though you can drop the pre-chorus if you had used it a number of times. Dropping a pre-chorus is done if you can go back to the chorus without the pre-chorus.

- Pre-chorus does not extend for more than eight bars

- Builds tension, thereby increasing the feeling of release in the chorus.

3. Listen to "This Kiss" to illustrate the use of the bridge. This song works for the following reasons:

- This song has three section with each section having a separate melody

- Each section has a different lyric meter which catches the listener's attention

- The pre-chorus consists of short lines with the last line showing a different lyric meter, signaling the chorus.

Kinds of song forms

- AAA – This song form is an old form with the simplest structure which is used in traditional folk music. Listen to "<u>The First Time I Saw Your Face</u>" – the song is an example of the AAA structure which consists of 3 repeated sections (verses) and moves with a slight variation towards the end to conclude the song. The AAA form is rarely used today since there is no chorus or bridge to hold the melodic interest. Another example you can listen to is Johnny Cash' "<u>I Walk the Line.</u>"

- AABA – this song form is a classic form with a long history behind it. Viewed as the ultimate song form, it is concise, short, seamless in its melody, and easy to remember. It is used on all styles of music and tempos, particularly in mid-tempo or slow ballads.

  Listen to two examples of this form: "Yesterday" by the Beatles and Billy Joel's "Just the Way You Are."

  Variations of this song form:

    - ABABAB (verse, chorus, verse, chorus, verse, chorus)

- ABABCB (verse, chorus, verse, chorus, bridge, chorus)

- ABABA (chorus, verse, chorus, verse, chorus)

- AABABB (Verse, verse, chorus, verse, chorus, chorus)

- ABCABC (verse, pre-chorus, chorus, verse, pre-chorus, chorus)

Guide for choosing a form

You may be one of those songwriters who get a flash of inspiration where the words and music come spontaneously. Some writers come up with the idea of a verse or chorus initially. But after the initial flash of inspiration, you will have to decide on a form to use to communicate your idea.

So, how do you choose which form to use for your song? Below are guides to help you select your form.

1) If you are starting with music, the tempo dictates the form. If your tempo is fast, choose a form with many sections, like ABCABCDC or AABABCB. These forms help you to sustain interest in your music. If you are writing a mid-tempo or a slow

ballad, choose either the shorter or the longer form.

2) When writing with the lyric first, the subject matter and the mood influence the tempo of the music. Imagine if you set the lyric of the Titanic theme "My Heart Will Go On" to a fast music? It would not work.

3) Another factor which affects the tempo is the ease with which the lyrics can be sung. You will encounter a problem when you try to use a lot of words, especially if the tempo is fast. The tongue may have difficulty saying all those words with a very fast tempo.

4) Consider the amount of words you need to tell your story. The AAA form is ideal in stretching, though it is not the choice of form if your purpose is commercial. A fast tempo with 3 or 4 sections can give plenty of space for your words and still have a strong musical interest.

Melody

Creating melodies is an art in itself. Though melodies found in classical and pop music have similarities, they differ in priorities. In classical music, melodic construction extends over a period of time. In pop music writing, musical ideas are short, repeated, and contrasted with less development. And, melodic lines lead to choruses and hooks in a short span of time.

The purpose of writing pop music is to repeat ideas with just enough contrast and variations to keep the listeners engaged with the song. The initial idea is the starting point of pop music's melody.

In a 4/4 time, the melodic line may run from a half measure to two measures. There may be instances where the melodic line occupies eight measures, like in a slow romantic ballad. For pop music, though, short melodic ideas are preferable since they are easy to remember.

Most songwriters get started with a flash of inspiration. Inspiration is a good place to start since what gets you subconsciously may also hook the others or the listeners. The challenge comes with expanding the idea into complete sections, then on to complete songs.

How to build a melody

You can learn to construct songs from your melodic lines using several techniques.

Repetition, contrast, variation and development

Look at this example below:

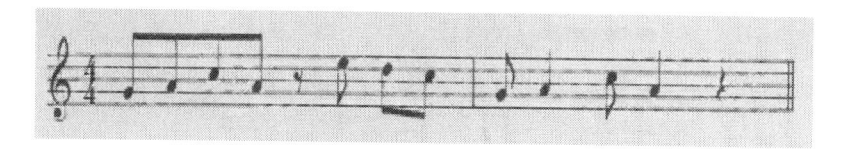

Then see how the notes in the first measure are repeated in the second:

You can expand the notes into four measures. However, it might sound too simple.

Be careful with mindless repetition though. If you are writing a song for commercial purposes, remember that there will be several stations playing your song again and again. Eventually, people will get bored listening to your song. To avoid boredom, try alternating two melodic ideas.

There are two ways in which you can use alternating melodic ideas. One is through variation, and the other is by contrast with both using repetition.

In the variation, the response phrase is slightly different from the original musical idea. The difference is slight and works to keep the melody from becoming too predictable.

In contrast, the response phrase is entirely different from the original musical idea. The close alternation of the two melodic phrases, however, links them fast in the listener's mind.

You can learn to use more complex melodic phrases by listening to songwriters who use sophisticated techniques for commercial writing. Songwriters like Burt Bacharach, Barry Gibb, and Michael MacDonald.

Guides to achieve contrasts in songs:

1. Changing levels of melodic line – Emphasize the more important section of your song by raising the pitch or changing the time values. For example, change your eighth or quarter notes to sixteenth notes. Or you can extend the length of your half notes.

2. Changing phrase length – If your verse is made up of short phrases, shift to long phrases (two measures or more), and vice versa. One is sure to get bored listening to a 4-line verse and followed by a 4-line chorus.

3. Changing rhythmic pattern – If your song has the same rhythm, break it with syncopation or vice versa.

4. Defining sections with appropriate transitions – In spoken and written language we use punctuations to indicate the tone of the sentence. In music, we also have punctuations to tell us where the song is at. Punctuations in music are achieved through a stop, a

build, a break, and a musical turnaround. Be careful, though, when making a jump to another section or you risk losing your listener. Lead your listener from one section to another carefully.

Vocal Range

A singer has a range of voice in which they can sing with consistency and professional control. You can make use of the voice range to make the songs you write more interesting.

The guide below will help you find the appropriate range for the different vocal abilities and song styles.

Modest range

This range is for the less-skilled singer, sing-along type of performer, and talk singer. Materials written for these types of singers should not go beyond their range. The range should be less than an octave.

Here is how an octave looks like on a staff:

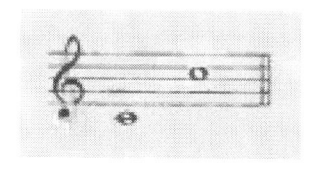

In music notes, an octave is a series of eight notes, with the first and the last note having the same name. The figure uses the example of C. You can have an octave on any note; if you start with D, you close an octave with the higher D.

Average range – The average range is the octave and three or four notes above. This range fits most pop singers and styles. You can have a few high notes or dramatic leaps, so long as they're not too demanding for the average singer.

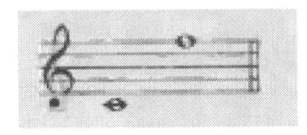

The figure above shows a range from C to a higher F (four notes above the octave.

Wide range – This range refers to an octave and five notes above and beyond. This range is appropriate for virtuoso singers or divas like Whitney Houston. There are, however, groups like the Boys II Men who can reach this range.

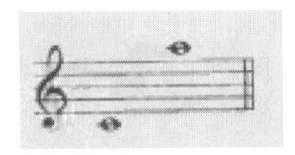

Scale context

A songwriter may use any key in writing a song. In fact, composers have made use of one or more scales in a composition, like Claude Debussy's L'Isle Joyeuse.

Debussy's composition, which is in the ternary+Coda form (A-B-A'-Coda), starts with the whole tone scale (figure a below), moves on to the A Lydian/Mixolydian scale mode in the next section (figure b), then on to the Diatonic A major scale, which resolves the instability caused by the A Lydian/Mixolydian scale (figure c below). The composition then returns to Coda and shifted to the diatonic scale.

Figure (a) is a whole tone scale with equally spaced notes (all in whole steps) and no tonal center which is characteristic of impressionist sound.

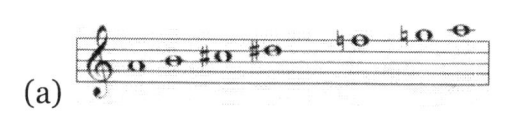

(a)

Figure (b) shows the A Lydian scale with the raised 4th scale degree (D#) and the lowered 7th scale (G natural) degree

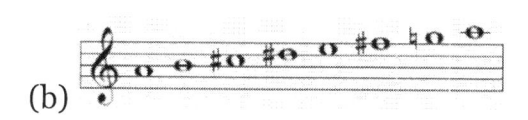

(b)

Figure (c) is in A diatonic scale which resolves the whole tone and the Lydian scales.

(c)

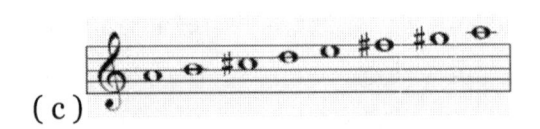

But, the actual tones in the scale used in the melody determine the style of the song.

Composers do not really think in terms of forms of a scale. But, how a composer uses and places a note and key intervals in the melody are the reasons for the pleasing sound of the scale, the natural flow of the melody within the scale, and the choice of chords selected naturally from the scale.

Harmony and Rhythm

Harmony is the combining of two or more pitched notes which sound pleasing and come up with a comprehensive whole. The result of the combination is known as chords. The quality of the chords used is what brings out the color and expression in the song. The imaginativeness in the use of chordal sound is what gives the song its distinctive appeal.

The concept of harmony applies to the building of chords, the qualities of chords, and chord progression. Note that harmony strictly applies to vocals and pitched instruments. Therefore, clapping and stomping, even when sounded together, is not harmony.

Harmony is one of the most crucial parts of a song, and can be difficult to get right. It is a central element in all types of songs – from the R&B, to folk music, to classical music. If you want to create music, it helps for you to have the skill and a solid grasp of chords and how you can use them to create your song.

Levels of chord construction

Playing 3 or more pitches at the same time produces a chord; you have created a harmony. You can create chordal sonoric beauty from a combination of intervals. The harmony you select would be determined by the level of sophistication your song requires.

For example, rock, folk and country style music uses simple chords or triads (a 3-note chord). Jazz is made up of more complex chords. Midway between the two you have the pop music and crossover music styles.

First level harmony

The most common is the major triad consisting of half steps which is made of major 3rd interval (4 half steps) and a minor 3rd interval above the first interval (3 half steps).

Another common triad used in pop music is the minor triad consisting of a minor 3rd interval and a major 3rd above the first interval.

You'll hear a third type of the first level triad used in rock music – the suspended triad (SUS). This triad is so-called because it suspends the 3rd and use instead a 4th. A suspended triad will have as its first interval 5 half steps (a 4th scale tone) and a major 2nd (2 half steps).

This is how a suspended triad looks like:

Csus2   Csus4

In the diagram above, the Csus2 has a major 2nd which means you include the D in the chord. The Csus4 means that the 4th note from C is found in the chord instead of the 3rd.

For songs using the triadic harmony chord progressions, listen to The Backstreet Boys' "I Want it That Way" and "Here Comes the Rain Again" by the Eurhythmics.

"I Want it That Way" uses three triadic chords F#m, D, A and the last chords E and A. "Here Comes the Rain Again" uses F, C and towards the end you hear D and G.

Second level harmony

Middle-of-the-spectrum triads are effective in R&B, country-pop, and MOR music. For this harmonic level, a 7th tone is added above the triads with the effect of a more polished and fuller sound, leading the listener to the song's resolution.

The formula for the 7th triad

- A dominant 7th chord consists of a major triad plus a minor 7th
- A minor 7th consists of a minor triad with an added minor 7th
- A major 7th chord has a major triad plus a major 7th added

Third level harmony

The third level harmony uses the 9ths, 11ths, and the more complex chord extensions. This harmonic level is mostly used in jazz-influenced harmonies, jazz-rock-fusion, R&B, and Broadway. This is a demanding harmonic level, which at this point, you need not concern yourself with.

How to create chord progressions

The art of harmonizing sounds is more than just selecting chords. It involves the flow of the chords and how they relate to the song's melodic shape and emotion. In other words, the flow of the chords or the chord progression is what determines the song's effectiveness.

In music theory, three fundamental principles govern the harmonic functions:

- Chords are collections of scale degrees of a particular key
- Each scale degree has its distinct tendencies
- The tendencies of the chords' scale degrees combined is the chord's function

You can build your chords in two ways: diatonically (the use of tones within a scale) or chromatically (the use of tones inside and outside the scale).

Diatonic chords

Diatonic harmony refers to notes or chords that relate to a certain key. For instance, the F tone relates to the C major scale. You may argue that F can be found in any other keys. You are right here, but it is only in the key of C that F is positioned as the 4th degree of the key of C. For a note or a chord to belong to a key, it has to be analyzed based on the degree of the scale.

There are two categories of diatonic groups: the primary and the secondary chords.

Primary triads express clear and unambiguous tendencies. The secondary chords are the minor triads which you find within the major scale. These secondary chords express a darker, serious shade of color and emotions compared to the primary triads.

Since the secondary triads are found within the same major scale, they support the primary triads and provide the contrast which makes the song interesting.

The use of secondary triads allow for a departure from a song's section without having to go far harmonically. For an example, listen to Cher's "Believe" and check the chorus section.

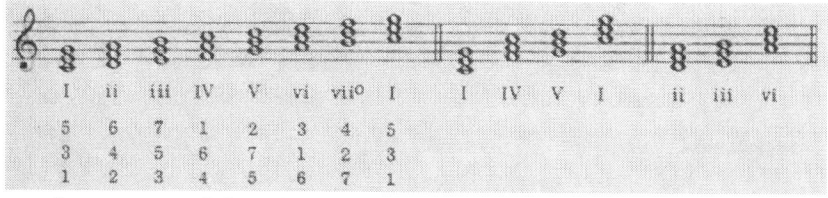

```
I   ii  iii IV  V   vi  vii°  I     I   IV  V   I     ii  iii vi
5   6   7   1   2   3   4     5     
3   4   5   6   7   1   2     3     
1   2   3   4   5   6   7     1     
```

In chapter 3 of this book, we learned that the notes in the scales are named. Roman numerals are one of the methods used to name the notes in the scale. Large numerals are used to indicate a major, for instance I indicates the first degree or the tonic of the scale and IV the 4th degree or the subdominant in the scale. A small numeral indicates a minor like ii which is the 2nd scale degree or the supertonic in the scale and vi the 6th scale degree or the submediant.

The second measure in the diagram above shows the three harmonic functions: the tonic (T), the subdominant (S), and the dominant (D). These names correspond to the degrees in the scale (refer to chapter 3 of this book on Scale Degrees) where the first degree is the tonic, the subdominant is the 4th degree and the dominant is the 5th degree.

Each harmonic function is made up of characteristic scale degrees. For the tonic, the characteristic scale degrees are 1, 3, 5, 6, and 7. The subdominant has 1, 2, 3, 4, and 6. Dominant's characteristic scale degrees are 2, 4, 5, 6, and 7.

In Cher's "Believe", the song makes use of the Primary triad I, IV, V combined with minor triads.

| I | V | ii | IV | I | V | ii | vi |

Horizontal chord construction

Not all songs are built out of vertical chords. Many contemporary songs use horizontal construction of melodies and supported with strong rhythmic background, bass lines, and countermelodies.

An example of horizontal construction of melodies is Ricky Martin's "Livin' La Vida Loca."

The melody starts with two triads, but followed by a melodic line. This phrase is repeated in the following measures. The melody is supported by a strong rhythmic beat and a bass line.

There are many means to use harmony to make your songs more interesting and effective. Imagine the chords as your coloring agents. Learn to discriminate between simplicity and sophistication of your harmonies that would match the kind of song you want to write.

It helps for you to be exposed to harmonic functions by listening to radio stations to become familiar with songs that mostly use triads, which ones play the 7th chord songs or the more complex ones.

One thing is certain: the more you get to know about chords, how they relate to each other and how they work, the more you become versatile in songwriting.

Groove

Groove is what musicians refer to as the feel of a song, the way it feels right. It is what gives music its rhythmic feel or swing. In jazz, you get to know the groove through its persistent and repeated pattern. It is the groove which comes as an unspecifiable character, but in a distinctive and regular way that draws the listeners in. Groove is understood in music as a rhythmic pattern that moves listeners to dance or tap the fee.

In technical terms, the groove is understood through the rhythmic elements of pulse, meter, tempo, syncopation, rhythmic subdivision, and texture.

The Rhythmic Elements

Pulse – refers to a regular and recurring beat. It is easy to detect a pulse in a march. In pop music, you get to know the pulse through the drum beat.

Tempo - refers to the rate of speed of the pulse. A slow ballad usually has 60 beats per minute (BPM). A mid-tempo song has 90 BPM, an up-tempo a 120 BPM, and a 150 BPM is in a hyper drive. For examples of each of the speed, listen to "I'll Make Love to you", a slow ballad. Listen to "Crazy for You" for mid-tempo speed, "Smooth" for up-tempo dance, and "Living La Vida Loca" for a hyper drive speed.

Meter – Meter is the way the beats are grouped into bars or measures. The most common type of grouping is the 4/4 time. In 4/4 time, four beats in a measure represented by a four quarter notes are grouped per measure. In a ¾ time, three beats or three quarter notes are grouped per measure.

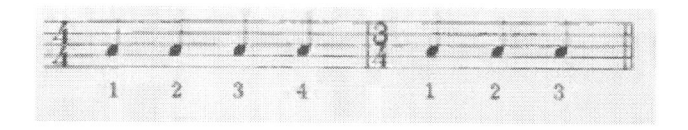

Rhythmic Subdivision – where a beat subdivides into smaller beats and thereby help define the style of the song.

a) A beat or a quarter note can be subdivided into two eight notes. Four quarter notes subdivided gives you 8 eight notes. You'll hear this type of rhythmic pattern in rock, MOR, and Latin dances and songs.

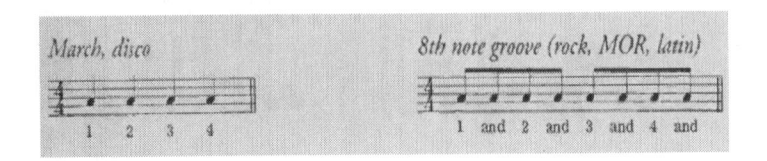

March, disco

1 2 3 4

8th note groove (rock, MOR, latin)

1 and 2 and 3 and 4 and

b) A quarter note may also be subdivided into four groups of triplets, such as in the diagram below and usually used in the 50s songs and the blues:

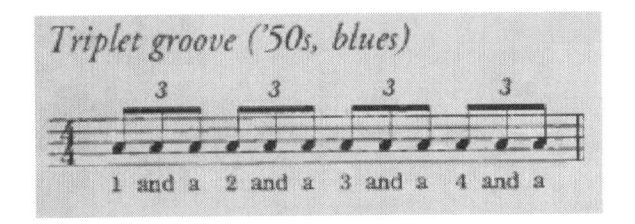

Triplet groove ('50s, blues)

3   3   3   3

1 and a 2 and a 3 and a 4 and a

c) The shuffle grove shows the quarter note subdivided into groups of triplets with an eighth rest between the end-notes of a triplet. This type is used in the 40s songs, country songs, be-pop, gospel, and blues.

Shuffle groove
('40s, be-bop, country, blues, gospel)

d) You can still subdivide the quarter notes into smaller beats, the 16th notes. The four quarter notes subdivided into the 16th notes will have four groups with four 16th notes each, as shown below. This grove is used for funks, reggae, R&B, and half-time rock.

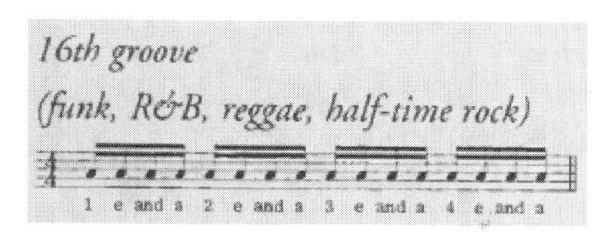

16th groove
(funk, R&B, reggae, half-time rock)

e) The swung is difficult to read and play. The quarter note is subdivided into a mix of eighth and sixteenth notes. This grove is used for hip-hop and rap.

Swung 16ths (hip-hop, rap)

The swung grove is usually notated as regular 16th notes to make it convenient for reading; it has an instruction above the first line. It gives the feel of an uneven and staggered rhythm.

f) The hybrid 16th over the 8th notes grove has four sixteenth notes in a pulse or beat over 2 eight notes. This grove is used in R&B, dance, and alternative music.

Hybrid 16ths over 8ths (dance, R&B, alternative)

g) The hybrid swung 16th over 8th notes you find in hip-hop and alternative songs.

Hybrid swung 16ths over 8ths (hip-hop, alternative)

Syncopation – where strong beats are found on weak notes. Another way to say it is that the rhythmic accents are placed on the weak inner beats of a measure. The effect of syncopation is to create a rhythmic drive.

An example of syncopated 8th note grove is the song "Smooth" performed by Santana. Look at the melodic line below:

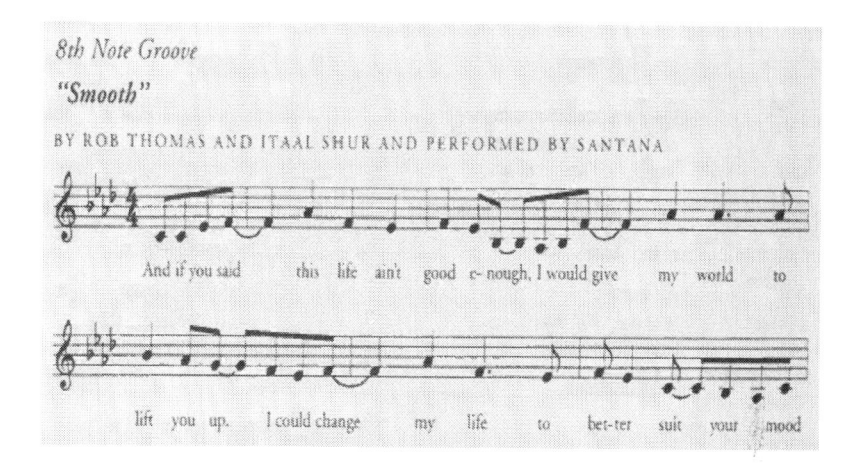

8th Note Groove

"*Smooth*"

BY ROB THOMAS AND ITAAL SHUR AND PERFORMED BY SANTANA

And if you said this life ain't good e-nough, I would give my world to lift you up. I could change my life to bet-ter suit your mood

It is usual to have the strong beat fall on the first note of a measure. But in "Smooth", the rhythmic accent falls on the second note of the second measure – the weak inner beat.

Texture – Texture in a song is determined by its sound and not the feel. The texture is how you combine melodic, harmonic, and the rhythmic materials in your composition to produce its sound quality.

Musicians usually describe the texture of the song in terms of its density, range, thickness, width between the lowest and the highest pitches. It is also distinguished based on the number of voices or parts and how these are related. For instance, a texture is said to be thick if the composition contains layers of instruments.

Types of texture

- Monophonic. This means having one voice and refers to a single melodic line. Several instruments can play a melody and fall under the classification of monophony if these instruments play one melodic line.

    The voices may be in different octaves or sing in unison and still be monophonic if they sing the same notes and move in the same rhythm. Monophonic texture is best exemplified by group singing, like "Happy Birthday."

    It is rare to see this kind of texture in modern songwriting.

- Homophonic. You find this texture common in Western music, both in popular and classical music. Homophonic texture has a single melody and one voice singing against the background accompaniment. The accompaniment may be played in simple chords or a melodic line. But, in either way, the melody is distinguishable.

Homophonic texture is common in pop, rock, and singer-songwriter music. This type of texture is ideal if you are new to songwriting.

- Polyphonic texture. This type is also known as counterpoint, indicating multiple voices independent of each other. These voices are of equal importance and are sung simultaneously. This texture is dense and complex, typical of the Renaissance and Baroque music.

Note that multiple voices do not necessarily mean multiple instruments. A keyboard or a guitar can play polyphonic music. Examples of this type of texture are the rounds, canons, and Bach's fugues.

Modern songwriting also makes use of polyphonic music. It is used in the complex form of songwriting, such as the Neo-classical Heavy metal and the progressive rock.

When listening to music of different textures, note that a song need not be classified under one category. Modern songs are additive; they may start as monophonic and develop into polyphony. An example of this developing texture is Whitney Houston's "I Will Always Love You."

Chapter 7. Writing the Lyrics of the Song

You may love writing poems and have thought of turning these poems into songs. Music is a most effective means of communicating ideas, and the words put into music make the message even more effective. Through the use of media channels, you are able to reach a wide spread of listeners.

A songwriter's approach, however, is much different from that of a poet or from any other type of creative writing. The element that is missing in poetry is the melody. But, it is also the melody that poses a challenge to a lyricist.

Lyrics are such that a vocalist is able to sing the words alongside the melody. There are techniques and principles to follow that would effectively call the attention of your listeners.

Simplicity

Simplicity in a song calls for saying something that everyone can relate to. For example, experiences that everyone has gone through, but do not know how to say it. You are writing a song, not only for yourself but for others to feel what you feel about life.

Often, a song fails to convey its message because of so many ideas the writer puts into the song, and not saying the ideas clearly add to the confusion. The trick is to focus on one idea and build the song around it. What you want to aim for when writing a song is to make your message clear to as many listeners as possible.

Songwriting is the ability to communicate your idea or feeling in an interesting, unique and enjoyable way.

Focus

The technique here is to capsulize your mental state or emotion in one word. For instance, feelings like happiness, love, hate, jealousy, and sadness. These are emotions people experience and feel. Any of these emotions can be the subject of your song. What you need to do is focus on specifics.

One of mistakes that most beginning songwriters make is to write down the first thing that pops into their heads, whether it is focused or not. This may be a good idea to begin with, but eventually, you have to focus on a single idea.

You may do a story on the emotion, or you may want to explore several aspects. For as long as you are writing about one emotion, you are on track. What is important is that you describe what the song is about.

An important factor to achieve focus is attitude. In songwriting, attitude refers to a strongly stated point of view. Songs like rap, hip-hop, and rock are strong in attitude. But, first-person songs of any style should also express an aggressive attitude. Listen to the song "[Something to Talk About](#)" to give you an idea of the element of focus. Another example is "[Independent Women](#)."

Titles

Titles are effective not only in catching the attention of the public but also in remembering the song.

A title, though, is not enough to make a hit of your song. There are titles that are imaginative but fail to catch the interest of the public. For a title to be effective, it should have a concept embedded in it. Having both a title and a concept is a great way to start to write the lyrics of a song. You will be amazed to find out that if you have the right title and concept, the song writes itself.

If you are able to write a short phrase for a title that incorporates a concept, it is easier to focus on your lyrics right from the start. Some fascinating song titles are

"Tears in Heaven", "Standing Outside the Fire", and "Cleopatra's Cat."

The concept embedded in your title is important. But, people will retain the title in their memory if you make your title catchy. A catchy title has any of the following features:

- A combination of attractive meter and a poetic device such as alliteration or assonance.

- Common phrases you hear every day, like "Knock on Wood" and "I Heard it on the Grapevine."

A title is also effective if it fits the music and supports the rest of the lyric.

When you have all the ingredients of a good title – catchy, conceptual, clever, and fits the music, you will succeed in making even the most mundane title become profound. Take the following songs as examples: "New York State of Mind" and "Georgia on my Mind."

In the songwriting journey, there will be times when a musical figure or the intensity of the emotion in the music suggests a title. This is a spontaneous process; when such happens, musicians set aside the intellectual approach and stay close to the emotional core.

When a mood suggests a title, put it in the first or last line of your verse or chorus. Repeat the title several times in the song and you can be sure people will remember it.

First lines

The first words and the first line of your song are critical. It is the first thing that a listener evaluates to determine whether he or she likes the song or not.

Your first line sets the tone of the song. It is what makes you want to listen to the end of the song. You can write an effective first line by asking the following questions:

- Where is the song taking place? Is it necessary in the song? What kind of a place is it? Are there features about the place worth writing about? If the place is a beach, the mountains, a country or a city, take care you are not describing a passing scene that carries no action, emotional charge, or attitude.

Here are some interesting examples of songs about a place: "Halfway into Heaven", "At Home in your Love", and "Ten Miles West of Houston."

- Can the season, day, or hour provide the flavor that increases the emotional impact of the song?

- If you are addressing someone in your song, is there something remarkable about the person you can say?

- If the song is about a person, can you say something that would give a picture of that someone or write a quick personality sketch?

- Can you use an active image?

If it is an emotion you are expressing, can you do it dramatically or poetically? Note, however, that the dramatic or poetic line you write depends on the tone you want to establish.

Rhyme

Most songs use rhymes, but the question is: why is rhyme important? And, what is it in rhyme that makes it work.

Rhyme and meter combined is crucial memory triggers. It's the reason we still remember our nursery rhymes.

Types of Rhyme

- Perfect rhyme - A rhyme is perfect when the stressed sound ending the line is identical with different preceding consonants. Example: action/fraction, god/quad, and variety/society.

The perfect rhyme is the most powerful rhyme to use. Try to use a perfect rhyme without changing the meaning of the line.

- Imperfect, slant, false, near, or half-rhyme - This type is common in pop music. It is close to rhyme but falls short, which is why there are those who argue that this should not be classed as rhyme at all.

However, there are times when you could not find a perfect rhyme to match your meaning, and you settle for a "near" rhyme, such as: around/down, port/fourth, and loss/wash.

- Masculine (also known as "one rhyme") - This type of rhyme is single-syllable where the last syllable rhymes. Examples: pack/rack and compromise/idolize.

- Feminine (or "two rhyme") - This type is a two syllable rhymes with the stress located on the first syllable. Here, the vowels and inner consonants match. Examples: masquerading/degrading and maker/shaker.

- Three rhyme - Rhyme is found in the last three syllables and the preceding consonants differ. Examples: facilitate/rehabilitate and medium/tedium.

- Open rhyme - Open rhyme is a rhyme that does not end in hard consonants. This type is used on held notes. Examples: fly/try and glow/snow.

- Closed or stopped rhyme - The type of rhyme that ends in consonants and pronounced with mouths closed, like b, p, d, q, k, and t. These words cannot also be sustained when sung. Take note of the "singability" factors when you write your songs.

- Internal, inner, or inside rhyme - This type may be easy to remember. End rhymes are at the end of the line while internal rhyme is found within the line.

Problems with rhyme

Songwriters often put more importance on rhyme than finding a compelling message to end the verse. It is like rhyming just to simply rhyme at the expense of making a statement. Rhyme over content or idea may be convenient, but this weakens the song.

Songwriters should avoid falling into this trap and instead to write several variations of the two initial lines and find an end word that provide rhyming possibilities.

If you are a beginner in songwriting, take caution of these vulnerabilities:

- Inversions

This method twists the order of words to end with a rhyme that would otherwise naturally occur at that point. It gives an awkward feeling. Look at this example:

I didn't think I was missed

Such bliss I felt you kissed

The example above is forcing the rhyme. Try reading "I felt such bliss when we kissed" and it would sound more natural.

- Identities

Strictly speaking, identities are not to be confused with rhymes. These use the same words, may have the same consonants preceding the end sound, and sounds that are identical but has different spellings (homonym), such as "crow" and "so".

This weak rhyming shows lazy writing. There are exceptions, though, like when you create parallel rhymes, like the example below which use *pout* and *shout* before the final word in the line:

I wanna shout about it

I'll just pout about it

There's no doubt about it.

Another acceptable rhyme is putting emphasis on a verse by repeating the variation of a line. For example, "Headin' down the valley, headin' all the way down the valley."

- Slang

Slang may be a popular source for rhymes, but you will have a problem if your song is recorded and played in the future. The slang today will sound alien tomorrow.

- Colloquial pronunciation

The problem caused by colloquial pronunciation is quite the same with slang. With this, you reduce the ability of the artist to perform the song. It is understandable for a songwriter to fit the song to a specific style, for instance the R&B or country songs.

The problem arises when the artist pronounce the word that is significantly generic in that style and sound awkward. Remember that you are writing a song that an artist can comfortably sing.

For instance, thing is sometimes sang as *thang* and rhymed with hang.

Exceptions to the rule

Writing in rhymes is a powerful tool in songwriting. There are, however, songs that don't have rhymes. Usually, these songs without rhymes are played by bands. Pop music also has songs without rhymes.

If you don't want to use rhymes and still get to communicate your ideas, you can do so. Remember, though, that rhyme is a powerful tool to remember your songs.

Songs without rhymes work because of the following reasons:

- They have exceptional melodies

- The lyrics are simple enough it is easy to remember

- The melody is so constructed that it does not need rhyme and meter or a rhyme expectation.

The rule in using a rhyme is to find the pairs or combinations while not disturbing the natural speech pattern flow; and, don't forget that you should not compromise the song's context and intended mood.

Poetic Devices

Poetic devices have been used by great poets throughout history. Songwriters of today use these devices to write great lyric. When we listen to songs of today, we are not aware of these devices. Still, we love the songs.

Know these devices and learn how to use them in your songs.

- Alliteration – this device refers to the repetition of accented consonants.

- Assonance – where the stressed vowels are in agreement but the preceding consonants differ.

- Similes – Similes are comparisons and they're characterized by the use of words such as "as" or "like. For instance, the phrases "sleeping *like* a dog" and "hard *as* rock" are similes. Be careful with using clichés. If you have heard the phrase before, try to look for a new one.

- Metaphor – a figure of speech which uses a phrase to represent something else. Metaphors are used to paint a colorful image. An example is "You are my sunshine."

- Allegory – a device writers use to turn an abstract concept into a concrete image. Paul McCartney's "Ebony and Ivory" is an example of this device.

McCartney used the black and white keys of the piano as an allegory to represent racial harmony.

- Personification – giving human characteristics to objects. An example: "When the ground started rolling, I heard the buildings scream."

- Hyperbole – this device uses exaggeration to drive home an idea. The phrase "You're a hurricane" is both metaphor and hyperbole.

- Irony – this device says the opposite of what is actually meant. It is also irony when you emphasize the incongruity of a situation. An example is playing the song "Silent Night" against the backdrop of news reports of violence in the streets.

- Antithesis – The use of opposing ideas (principle of contrast) to emphasize a point. Used in songs, antithesis heightens the dramatic tension (of a decision), or express a strong emotion. An example is a line in the song by The Clash, "Should I *stay* or should I *go*." Another example is the song by the Temptations "My Girl" where the song goes – "I've got *sunshine* on a *cloudy* day."

- Characterization – the creation or construction of a character that is convincing. When building a character or an image, try to write a lot more that says about the character or the situation. A great example of characterization is "Shower" by Becky G. Or listen to Michael Jackson's "Billy Jean" and John McCartney's "Eleanor Rigby."

Prosody and Meter

Prosody looks into the patterns of rhythm and sound as used in poetry. Its concern is determining the length and shortness of syllables and how these syllables form into rhythmic patterns or meters. And, it is used in the writing of lyric and dramatic verses.

In songs, prosody is the agreement of music and lyric. There are factors that affect the quality of your prosody, such as:

- If the lyric has a happy or positive message, don't match it with a melody that is in the minor key. Minor chords depict despair, longing, loss, and pain. Major keys are more on a happy tone.

- Be alert for word combinations that can be heard as other words. For example, the phrase "What do I know?" may be heard as "What a wino?" Another is this phrase "Let the winds take hold" and is heard as "Let the wind stay cold."

- Be careful with adjacent words beginning or ending with the same sound. For instance the words "teach children" or "strange journey". Your artist will have a hard time saying the words, particularly if the tempo is fast. The rule is for you to make certain that your listener hears what you want them to hear. And make sure that your artist can sing what you write.

A way for you to know if your lyric sings well is for you to sing them as you write the words, and sing them at the tempo you intend for your song. Note that words on paper are different when performed. You may feel comfortable singing the words at a slow speed, but what happens when you increase the tempo? If the words don't feel right in your mouth, don't hesitate to change them.

An important tool that supports prosody is the lyric meter. The use of this tool allows you to highlight the natural speech pattern and fits right into the musical pulse and melody.

Prosody is necessary to understand the emotional content of your lyric. This is where knowledge of prosody as used in prose and poetry comes in handy to you as a songwriter. You can review prosody here briefly.

Metric meter is the grouping of stressed and unstressed words and syllables. The symbols used to indicate the stressed (′) and unstressed (˘) syllables or words are referred to as the scansion notation. A single line (|) marks the division between metric feet.

The basic unit in prosody is the foot. The following are the forms of foot:

FORM	DESCRIPTION
Iamb (iambic)	Unstressed syllable followed by a stressed syllable
Trochee (trochaic)	Stressed syllable followed by an unstressed syllable
Dactyl (dactylic)	Stressed syllable followed by two unstressed syllables
Anapest (anapestic)	Two unstressed syllables followed by one stressed syllable
Spondee (spondaic)	Two stressed syllables together
Pyrrhic	Two unstressed syllables together
3-SYLLABLE FEET	
Tribrach	Three unstressed syllables
Amphibrach	Unstressed- stressed-unstressed

Below is the visual representation of the forms of prosodic foot.

Name of Foot	Scansion	Examples
iamb	˘ ´	in-sáne, good-bý, to-níght, for good
trochee	´ ˘	héal-thy, lóv-er, mó-ney
anapest	˘ ˘ ´	go-ing óut, ma-king sénse, un-der-stánd
dactyl	´ ˘ ˘	pó-e-try, úl-ti-mate, I'm ó-kay, you're ó-kay
spondee	´ ´	dówn-tówn, stár-shíp, héad-lóng
amphibrach	˘ ´ ˘	be-líev-ing, con-cérn-ing, I lóve it

The emotional strength of a song depends on the meter you choose. Each metric foot has a color distinct from the others. The spondee exudes a deliberate feeling. The

Iambic has a sense of seriousness. The anapest is light in character, and therefore, will not work in a heavy subject matter.

Prosody is necessary to understand the emotional content of your lyric. The discussion in this chapter is only the beginning of your journey in writing lyrics. If you are serious with being a songwriter, you may need to read more on the subjects just discussed. But, a better and faster way to learn is to write and write songs.

Chapter 8. The Pull of Song Hooks

It used to be that a single hook is enough for the whole song. Now it appears that you need a hook for each section of a song. And, people today appear to have short attention span. The average they give a radio channel is seven minutes before they switch to another channel.

Unless, a song is able to grab the attention of the listeners, it is unlikely they will stick to the end of the song. This is what a hook does – grab the attention of listeners to your songs. You need a hook to hold catch the people's attention and entice them to listen to your song again and again.

What Is A Hook?

The term hook is best used in commercial songwriting. It is what sticks in your memory after the song is over. It is that part of the song which catches your attention, and once it does, you can't help but sing it.

A hook is a musical idea used to make the song appealing. Songwriters often use various techniques to establish a hook. These techniques may include any or a combination of the following: skips with the range of an octave, use of interesting lines, or use of rhythmic syncopation, instrumentation, and vocal timbre.

There are, however, hooks that do not contain any unusual element. An example is the song "Be My Baby". The hook is in the phrase "be my baby" juxtaposed over a chord progression in the chorus section.

Most songwriters, especially those writing for commercial purposes, use hooks to make hit songs. If you are one of these songwriters, remember that hooks can complement each other, but it can also compete with each other. So, be careful how you construct and use your hooks.

Know that hooks are genre dependent. The effectiveness of your hook also depends on its placement in the song. A hook fails in its function more because the emphasis placed on a hook in its context is less. It is the task of the songwriter to build appropriate hooks and placed in appropriate parts or sections.

Another thing to remember about constructing hooks is that it needs diligence. Making hit songs don't come by luck. Songwriting is an art and a craft. A diligent songwriter has to craft the song, needs to know and understand the components of the song, and know how to put them all together in such a way that it works to the satisfaction of both songwriter and public.

The question is: What make hooks great and lead to hit songs?

Characteristics Of Great Song Hooks

Your average listeners may not always know what a hook is. What they know is that they like the song and somehow becomes fixated with it. But, for songwriters, knowing and understanding song hooks can greatly help them with their future compositions and recordings.

Below are some qualities that you find in great song hooks:

1. Hooks are short. They usually span from one beat to eight beats. Longer than eight beats and it becomes difficult to retain the song in memory.

2. Catchy melodic shape. The hook in the melody combines a stepwise move and a leap, the change succeeds in pulling the attention of the listener back to the song.

3. A combination of melody and catchy rhythmic pattern. A catchy rhythm has to be simple for easy recall, but contains an element of new or unique element, like the use of syncopation, to build a groove. An example is Deep Purple's "Smoke in the Water."

4. Hooks often disappear at different parts of the song. Dropping a hook at a certain section and

bringing it back makes the song more appealing. Listen to "Superstition" and you hear the clavinet played from the beginning of the song until it was dropped in the part that sings "when you believe in things you don't understand."

5. Having a strongly developed motive does not necessarily mean a strong hook. A hook is only one of many other techniques to lure people. Know the difference between a motif (or theme) and a hook.

A Motif Is Not A Hook

Many songwriters mistake the motif as the hook. This is understandable since motif is related to the hook. And, a motif is also a short fragment, just like the hook.

While hook and motif are both short, hook is a musical idea while the motif is the building block of the melody, a starting point to develop a melody. A motif can serve as the source of other ideas in the song.

Motif works in the background, while the hook is up front. The hook needs to be up front if it is to do its job of grabbing the attention of people. The listeners are not usually aware of the use of motif in the song, though they hear it repeated in different pitches. In some songs, the motif appears as the basic rhythm laid down by the drummer.

Some examples of motifs for a song might be the basic rhythm that the drummer lays down, then some melodic shapes that show up in the melody which might also be picked up by the rhythm guitar.

Another difference between motif and hook is that a hook is repeated in much the same way during the duration of the song. The motif is an idea that is developed and modified as the song goes on.

The important difference of the two is in its function. The hook has a compelling power that pulls the listeners back to the song. The motif has the power to strengthen the song's structure as it pulls all elements of a song together.

It makes no sense to say that one is more important than the other. Both serve and support a song in different ways.

Types Of Hooks
Structural hook

This hook forms part of the song's structure, like the hook chorus. The hook chorus repeats for several times and contains the title of the song, often in the first or last line of the chorus.

Instrumental hook

These are melodic phrases that are not part of the vocal melody, but remains in our memory like the melody. It is a catchy melodic phrase without lyric that is repeated throughout the song. There are times when an instrumental hook is the heartbeat of the song.

Listen to the Beatle's "Something" to have an idea of what an instrumental hook sounds like.

Story line hooks

This is the kind of hook where you may not remember the melody but the story remains in your memory. Often, the story is so evocative and powerful such that the memory stays far longer than the melody. An example of this type of hook is "Goodbye Earl" by Dixie Chicks.

Production hooks

With the help of sophisticated recording technology and instrumentation, songwriters are now able to write production hooks for their songs. Modern technology has made possible experimentation of how various instrumentation sounds when combined. And, phrasing and flanging are now incorporated into electronic boxes that can be activated by a tap of a button.

Specific sound evokes specific emotional response. This feature can be maximized, together with the melody and the lyric, to create the desired emotion and mood.

A sound that has not been heard before is an effective hook. Take care though that you don't get carried away with sound experimentation that you forget what really matters – that the song is still the most important thing.

Signature hooks

These are hooks introduced at the beginning of the song. It is a melodic motif – a musical phrase - that is easy to remember and positioned at the beginning of the song. The signature hook can also be placed in the turnaround, which is the interlude between the end of the first chorus and the next verse.

Non-lyric vocal hooks

Non-lyric vocal hooks are sounds that create strong hooks when linked to appealing melodies, such as "ah", "ooh" "hey", and "oh." An example of this hook is Lady Gaga's "Bad Romance." Another example is the use by the Beatles of "yeah, yeah, yeah" in their song "She Loves You."

Catchy rhythm hooks

Many songwriters use catchy and unique rhythm as a strong hook, like syncopation. Or using a pause or a stop is an unusual hook element you can use, like the iconic hit of the Supreme's "Stop! In the Name of Love." Also listen to Jason Mraz's single "The Remedy" for an example on the use of syncopation as a hook.

Guide to writing hooks

You might believe that you know how to write songs and have assimilated this knowledge such that lyric and melody comes to you spontaneously. But, it takes more than a lyric and melodic sense to create hit songs.

But what if, despite what you believe to be a great musical content of your song, you fail to hold the attention of your listeners long enough to mark it in their memory?

So, how do you create hooks that work for you? Here are a few tips to help you write hit songs.

1. Repeat the hooks. Contrary to what many songwriters believe, the chorus is not the only place you can position your hook. For maximum memory recall, place your hook in the beginning and towards the end of your song.

    By repeating the hook, it gains power and distinguishes it from the rest of the song's lyrical content. Also, people tend to retain in their memory what they hear first and last.

    Just be careful not to overdo it, otherwise people will get tired of hearing your song. With practice and exposure, you will get the right balance of hook placement and repetition in your songs.

2. Vary the rhythm. This technique is effective in re-engaging your listeners back to the song. You can change the rhythm in your verses and the choruses. You can vary the rhythm by:

    - Breaking up the words in your hook to make it interesting
    - Inserting changes in tempo, syncopation, rhythm
    - Adding an effect like non-vocal lyrics or stuttering. Listen to "Changes" by David Bowie where the performer sang changes as ch-ch-changes and makes the line catchy.

    You can also pause or stop before the hook or before a word you think needs emphasis. Silence is also an effective way to catch people's attention.

3. Try not to overshadow the hook. Having multiple lines in the chorus that are different from the title will drown your hook.

    A hook is about a single musical idea that keeps repeated in the song. Multiple lines will create problems for you. People will have to know about your song to request it and find it online and to spread it— the name or a fragment of the lyrics.

You also have to consider a DJ or a radio program manager. If they know and recognize the hook in your song, they will know when to insert your song into their cycles and when to promote it.

If you are having difficulty setting up your hook, you can pick the strongest line from your song and repeat it. You can also use the line in your verse or bridge.

4. Choose words with care. Do not repeat words from the hook in other sections of your song. For instance, if you have the word "home" in your song, don't use it again in other parts. Instead, use synonyms or conjure clear images related to the word. If your listeners have heard the word before your hook, it won't have the desired effect, and they will tune out.

    Your word will have power if it has personal meaning to you. What has meaning for you will resonate back to your listeners.

5. The high point should be your hook. This trick is what is referred to as the *money note*. This is the note that pulls the listeners back to your song because of the high pitch or is held longer than the

other notes. Combining the money note with your hook gives you the assurance of a hit song.

When you use this technique, make it sound natural and not forced. Try to speak the lyrics; you will notice they consist of a certain pitch and meter. You might also find out that the word you want emphasized with a high note does not need the highlight. It might just be another word in the line.

Chapter 9. What you Need to Know Before Writing Your Song

Budding songwriters dream of becoming professional songwriters. They like to write songs, not just any song, but songs people would love and remember. It is not, however, easy to create melodies that appeal to people and pull them magnet-like. Even experienced songwriters, at one point or another, go through a writer's block.

The process of writing songs is not the same for all songwriters. Each songwriter makes use of different approaches in writing songs. If you expect to have a formula for writing songs, you will be greatly disappointed.

A formula for songwriting won't work because of several factors. The taste of people in music differs a lot. The taste also changes over time. And, there are several elements involved in creating songs. These elements are knowledge of music and its language, instruments, lyrics, and an understanding of yourself and people.

There are, however, tips you can use and steps you can take in your effort to compose your songs. They can help you in a big way, especially if you do not know where to start.

Where to start creating your song

Getting started is almost always the most difficult part of writing songs. Some songwriters start with a title, while others start with the melody. Still, others consider writing the chorus as the best place to start.

Other approaches used by songwriters are to start with a hook, use of a killer intro first in the hope that this will lead naturally to the other parts of the song, and starting with the lyrics and get to the tune afterwards.

As mentioned earlier, there is no fast rule in writing songs. So, don't worry much over where to start. Getting started boils down to the songwriter, the inspiration, and the song that will determine the starting point.

Lyrics matter

If you are composing for instrumental music, then there is no reason to worry over lyrics. But, if you are writing a song, then the lyric is crucial to your song.

Writing the lyrics can be most frustrating and difficult part in songwriting, especially for one who is a beginner and lacks the experience.

A good start is to have a clear idea about your song. Write down exactly what you want to say in your lyrics. When you have written down your message, experiment with the rhythm, cadence, and structure of the words to fit your melody.

A strong lyrical hook for the chorus is important. You can then build the bridge and verses around the central idea.

Record your moment of inspiration when it comes.

It is so frustrating to come up with a melody and not being able to recall it later. It is, therefore, necessary for you to take note of your idea while it is still fresh in your memory.

You can record it on your phone or scribble a note on your pad or on a scratch paper, whichever is handy. You will appreciate doing so when it comes for you to continue with your song.

Write from your experience

Listen to different kinds of music. You will find that many great songs are about personal experiences. Artists often draw from personal experiences, traumas, and real life events to spark the creativity within them.

Use your hard times or great times experiences for song impact. Make use of these feelings and put them into songs you can be proud of.

Don't be afraid to collaborate with other musicians

Collaborating with other musicians often helps, especially when you suffer from writer's block. It is a great way to find your new ground, start afresh, and on a different perspective.

Tell them how far you are with your song, discuss ideas they suggest, and be open for what comes out of the discussion. You may be amazed how an outside perspective can help you on your track and bring the best out of your song.

Keep your song simple and build on it.

Keep your song simple, initially. This is an outstanding way to speed up your songwriting process and to build the structure of your song.

Many complex songs started simple – a few chords played on a keyboard or guitar. Once you have a hold on the basis of the song, it is easy to add instruments to your melody or other music elements later. By overdoing your song at the start, you are making it harder for yourself to complete the song.

Take breaks every now and then.

Writing a song can be mentally tiring, more so if you are struggling with the flow of ideas. A 15-minute break from what you are doing can help recapture that creativity in you and keep it flowing again.

Don't allow your mind to become clouded such that you fail to see the ideas and inspiration you are after. The length of time you write the song does not matter much. What is important is the song – your final product.

Don't overdo your thinking.
You are your worst critic. Judging your own songs harshly will not get things done. It is necessary that you keep an open mind. You might think it better to take your time with your writing and to go over each part of your song, but you are actually making it hard on yourself. Stop worrying and let the creative process flow.

Overthinking is your worst enemy. What you need to do is to get the basis of your song so you can get back to it and change it later, should you find it necessary.

Welcome feedback.
After hours of working, you tend to lose sight of the quality of your song – how good or how bad your song is. Find a trusted someone who can give you an honest advice, someone whose opinion you value and ask for their opinion of your song. You might be surprised with the insights they give on how you can improve your work.

Don't go for those who are afraid to be honest with you and hurt your feelings. They won't be able to contribute much to your song.

Don't be afraid of failing.

Successful songwriting comes from a combination of hard work, talent, and positivity. If you struggle and feel you are failing in your effort to write a song – don't give up. Instead, keep going. Learn from what Johnny Cash said about failure –

"You build on failure. You use it as a stepping stone. Close the door on the past. You don't try to forget the mistakes, but you don't dwell on it. You don't let it have any of your energy, or any of your time, or any of your space."

Chapter 10. Write Your Song with These Easy-to follow-Steps

If you have reached this part of the book, then you are ready to try and make your own song. You have the tools and techniques of the art and craft of songwriting. What you need to do now is to apply them to your songs.

It is, however, understandable if despite what you have imbibed from your reading the chapters, you harbor some doubts and ask yourself questions. You might waver between starting with a melody first or with the lyrics. And, you hesitate if your completed song is good or bad.

Take this hint: if your song is a genuine expression of your feelings, then it is a good song. What others think of your song should not concern you. If your song communicates your feelings and moves people emotionally, then your song has the potential to become a hit.

To overcome your hesitation, you can follow the steps below and do some exercises. One key to success in writing songs and feel good about your song is to practice, practice, and practice.

Start With The Title

We mentioned earlier that there are several approaches to start writing a song. But, if your question is which approach to use that would be appropriate for you, starting with a song title can prod you on.

The importance of the title

Some songwriters start with the title for the following reasons:

- An appealing title is usually what listeners remember

- It is the defining line of the song. It tells what the song is about.

- It serves as your guide to keep you on track with your work and keep your listeners tuned in to your song

You can start with a title which appeals to you most. If you like the feel and sound of your title, chances are your listeners will, too. Be sure that the title makes you want to know more about it.

How to find good titles

When thinking of a title, choose action words, short phrases, or images that have energy in it. Check the newspaper headlines and you can get ideas from them.

Another trick is to be alert with dialogues when you are watching television. There could be lines that capture your attention and make it a source for your title. Or you can listen to your friends and family for interesting phrases. A good source for title is your Self. Tune in and listen to yourself and do stream-of-consciousness writing.

Write down the possible titles you find and write them fast without judgment. Go back over the list and look for good phrases. Make this list the first of possible titles for your song.

Do this as an exercise: mix and match words from phrases in your list, substitute listed phrases with your own words, and play with the ideas to come up with a possible title. Try to find one phrase you feel can develop into a song. Mark or encircle the selected phrase so you can return to this phrase later.

Turn the title into a lyric

When you have your title, start making a lyric out of it. You can do this by asking questions about the title. Your questions will help you finish your work and make the song say what you want to say.

Every song title is suggestive of questions. These questions are the ones you want to explore, or they may the questions your listeners have. Answer both and you have a good start for creating the lyric.

You can these ask these questions:

- What is the meaning of your title?
- How do you feel about the title?
- What is happening to or in the title?
- Who are involved?
- Why is the title important?

You can choose your own questions or add more to the ones above. And, try to anticipate questions your listeners may have.

Do this: Go back to the list and the title you marked. What questions can you ask about the title? Write the questions and include what you want to say about the title. When you have done these, ask questions you expect the listeners will ask and write them down.

Answer your questions and try to keep them short. Eight to ten words are acceptable; more than these numbers and you won't be able to use all the words. These Are Raw Materials So You Can Explore As Many Possibilities As You Can.

Choose Your Song Structure

When you have your lyric, you can start choosing your structure. But before you can choose a song structure, it is best to be familiar with the song parts, the better to maximize its use for your song.

The role of song parts

Let's take a look back at the song parts discussed in a previous chapter 6, only this time, we'll be mentioning the concept of breaks as well. These sections are discusses so you'll have some starting point on what kind of approach to use when writing the lyrics depending on the role of that particular part.

<u>Intro</u>

The name explains itself – it is the introduction to the song. This is an important part of the song, but most often taken for granted. This is because the introduction is viewed as an arrangement and not the composition.

The intro, however, is the first thing the listeners hear. Many songwriters use the intro to establish the tonality or the groove of the song that is to follow. It may consist of a chord or chord progression that is related to, but different from, the main idea.

It is the first statement of primary importance that should be able to catch the attention of your audience from the start. Otherwise, it is easy for them to move on to something else.

So, make sure to come up with a killer intro since it has the potential of making your song easily recognizable.

Verse

This part sets the context, characters, and setting of the song. A well written verse, therefore, gives the listeners the idea of what the song is about. And, it also supports the chorus, which contains the main idea, moving the song forward.

The verse develops the story of the song and entertains the listeners. The experienced songwriters manage to write verses which change the meaning of the chorus after each verse. This technique is what makes a song mind-blowing. You can also learn this technique with practice and experience.

The point is to explore the emotions and intellect of the listeners.

The verse is usually made up of two segments which spans to eight bars each. This technique allows you to feel creative, different with each verse while unified by the main idea. You can vary your melodies, chord progressions, and harmonize taking your listeners higher until you reach the chorus.

The Pre-chorus or Lift

This part prepares the listeners and builds anticipation for the chorus. The pre-chorus serves as a teaser which allows you to increase the impact of your chorus through its delayed appearance. And, it serves as a signal to an incoming transition.

Often, the pre-chorus is made up of 4 or 8 measures. Where a pre-chorus appears in the first verse, it then appears in each subsequent verse. Where there are 2 verses before the chorus, the pre-chorus usually appears only in the verse right next before the chorus.

The lift or pre-chorus is created by varying the volume or rhythm or by creating tension with the use of contrast. This part may be repeated with the same lyric or melody, ending with an unresolved melody. But, you will also hear songs where the melody of the pre-chorus remains constant while the lyric changes each time. An example of this type is "You Belong With Me" by Taylor Swift.

Chorus

Chorus is also referred to as the Refrain. It is the most important part of the song. AS mentioned earlier, the chorus contains the main idea of the song and is that part which is easily retained in memory.

It is this idea that is repeated lyrically, melodically or musically. This part is what the listeners are waiting for, and should be the best part of your song. And, this is the reason why it is used interchangeably as the hook.

As an example, listen to Fireflies by Owl City and see how the chorus' role changes through the song.

The Bridge

This is the part that breaks the song's repetitiveness, adding an element of surprise to it. It presents a new and different angle to the main idea.

The usual way to add surprise is to change to a relative key using the same key signature. Often, the bridge is made with a different melody, rhythm, and chords with the effect of experiencing contrasting emotions.

Another way of making a bridge is to play from 8 to 16 bars a solo instrument. Often, the soloist improvises. Be careful with having the soloist play too long since the listeners may be holding their interest out of respect to the soloist. Too long and they tune out.

The Break

Some musicians believe that the bridge and the break is the same but they actually aren't. Well, a bridge is regarded as a break of sorts because it's also usually a short section, but for many musicians , these two aren't the same.

A break is a short section of the song which usually appears between verses. This is a brief pause or rest in a song functions to add excitement and dimension. It usually uses an instrument playing solo, percussion, silence, or a combination of these materials.

A **bridge** is (music) is also a short section but it transitions from one part of the song to another without any pause.

Our brains easily pick out sound patterns, and what breaks that pattern effectively grabs our attention. The breaks are the unexpected moments in a song that entertain our brains. Listen to "Call Me Maybe" by Carly Rae Jepsen and be alert for the breaks which occur before the chorus goes back to the verses.

Note that the break is optional. You are not required to have them in your song.

Outro

This refers to that part that ends the song. An outro may use an instrument, a brand new part, or a tag to end the song.

The ideal song structure for today's listeners

You came across the kinds of structure in Chapter 6 of this book. There are several song forms you can choose from. But, you may want to consider the AABA form.

The AABA (verse, verse, chorus, verse) is a classic song form and considered as the ultimate song form since you can use it in all styles of music and tempo.

There are many variations to this classic AABA form, and the one common to contemporary hit songs is the ABABCB (verse, chorus, verse, chorus, bridge, chorus). This song form is preferred by listeners because it has enough repetitions to make the song familiar and a variation to hold their interest.

Recall that the verse has the same melody but differs in lyrics. The lyrics provide the information, such as people, situation, or emotions. The chorus may be repeated three or more times in a song using the same lyrics for each repetition. The chorus captures the essence of the song. Often, the title of the song appears in the chorus.

The bridge has a different melody, chord progression, and lyrics from the verse and chorus. It serves as your break from the repetition of verse and chorus.

Do this: Go back to the questions you wrote about the title. Choose one question to answer in for section in the song. Remember that the chorus gets to be repeated several times, so the most important question goes to this section.

Make sure that the question is answerable by an emotion. And, use your title in the chorus. When you are done with your chorus lyric, continue with your verse lyric. Verse lyrics are more conversational, so keep the lyrics simple, honest, and open.

How to choose the appropriate song structure

While the form AABA and the variation are recommended here, it is not always that this form fits all songs you are likely to make. So here are a few tips you can do to choose the best form for your song. Ask yourself the following questions when struggling with what song form to choose.

1. How does it feel? Pay attention to the feel of the song. Listen to the vibe, the groove, and the emotion of the song.

Does it feel like an epic song? You can try the verse-chorus with a bridge structure. An example you can listen to is the song "Fix You" by Coldplay. If it is a mellow song, try doing the verse-verse form and use rich lyric as the refrain. If you feel you have a lot to say related to the main idea, try the verse, pre-chorus, chorus, and bridge form.

What is important is for you to feel the song and find the form that matches it.

2. What is the idea of the song?

The idea can suggest the structure of your song. If your song has characters and a storyline, you may want to try a form that helps the story flow through the song, such as the all-verses form.

If you are writing a sad song like a breakup song, have the main lament in your chorus and make the verses support the chorus.

What is important is for the structure to elevate the story in your song.

3. Does it sound natural?

Feel the song in the structure and see if it feels right to you. If you try it with different song forms, what feels the most natural to you? Where is the song taking you?

If you feel that the song needs to build, have it in a chorus or an epic bridge. If you sense that the song needs to mellow out, have it as a refrain at the end of the verse.

What we want to say is, go with your instinct. Your instinct may be right.

It helps to know the form and parts of a song for you to create a hit song. But, what really matters is what your guts or instinct have to say. It all boils down to the songwriter – to your musical taste and preference. All you need do is to be confident with yourself and your craft.

Bring Life To Your Song Through Images And Action Words

The ideas, images, and action words are your raw materials for the song you are trying to create. Give life to your song through these raw materials.

Look at your title and try to conjure images and words the title suggests. Write them down. Make the words and images specific to make the picture you want to paint clear for the listeners. Avoid being abstract in your portrayal of an image. Like *happy* is a bit abstract. How can you portray *happy* in your song? A trip to the beach is an example of being more specific with "happy." You can be more specific and say what it is in the beach that makes you happy.

Another example is the word changes in it. Ask yourself questions like: what are changes happening? What would be the effect of these changes to a person? Who is this person experiencing the change? Listen to David Bowie's "Changes" and these questions are answered in the song? See what images were used to bring out the emotional effect of changes.

Write down what comes into your mind and avoid evaluating what you wrote at this point. It is possible that you are not going to use all that you wrote. But, they present possibilities which you can use for your song.

Do this: Make a list of images, ideas, and words or phrases related to the title. Don't mind about rhymes or making sense of the words or phrases at this point. Also, avoid being critical of the ideas and continue writing them as they come to you.

When you are done writing down ideas, think of contrasting words, images, ideas, and phrases. Write as many as you can in each column and allow yourself to follow the trail. This exercise is best in bringing out the creativity in you.

When you think you have enough words or imagery, try putting them into your verse and chorus lyrics. Review what you have written. Replace those lines with action words that help bring out the emotion in your song.

Look For The Melody In Your Lyrics

We never examine the changes in the sound of the words we speak. But, the pitch of our voice changes when we speak. To an extent, we are actually "singing" a melody each time we speak. Otherwise, if we speak in a monotone, we end up like a robot speaking.

Every time we converse with someone or speak in public, we use the elements of pitch, rhythm, volume, and phrasing – the elements of a song. In a song, these elements become exaggerated or emphasized. It is, therefore, a good idea for you to speak your lyrics and get started with a melody.

The melodic part of the speech conveys the emotion of the speaker. By changing the melody, the words assume a different meaning. Try saying "Oh" with different punctuation marks and you'll see the difference of emotions conveyed.

Use this melody in speech to give added emotional impact to your songs. If your lyric is asking a question, try moving your voice up towards the end of the melody. It will feel like asking a question.

Do this: For a conversation tone, like in your verse, speak your verse lyric casually, like in a conversation. Then you can exaggerate a little to begin creating your melody. Exaggerate the ups and downs in your and keep the pauses that occur naturally in a conversation. You can make the changes later.

Again, these are just raw materials. You can explore many possibilities with the voice changes and note the emotions the changes convey.

For the chorus, this part usually contains urgency and energy. It has the heart of the song and is usually done with a higher voice range. Therefore, put as much emotion as you can into your chorus. Exaggerate the pitches, but keep the rhythm and the pauses as they come naturally.

When you have the melody suggested in your lyric, trying singing the melody with an accompaniment, like a guitar or a keyboard, and play with the chords.

Continue to work on your melody and lyrics using the technique just mentioned. Gradually smooth and change until you land on something you like. Then, move on with the rest of the lyric until you reach the final melody.

Chapter 11. Get into the Songwriting Business

Writing great songs is not the end of your journey. You might think that the business side of music is not for you, and you get someone to take care of promoting and selling your songs. They leave their creations for others to handle the business, only to regret later because of sad experiences brought upon by ignorance.

The songs you create and the talent that went into their creation are your babies. You would want to know how your songs fare out in the world and that they get every advantage they deserve. As your creations, you would want to protect them.

The desire to protect your songs while sharing them with the public may urge you to have a publishing company market your songs. Or you may be inclined to become your own publisher.

How To Protect Your Songs

It is natural for you – as the creator – to feel attached to your song. You have, however, to see your creation as a commodity, an *intellectual property*.

It is accepted – worldwide – that an artist has the right to keep ownership of his or her creations. The law protects the artist's rights and that the artist can expect compensation from those who would want to copy the work.

The songwriter may also assign the rights to the songs to a publisher for purposes of recording the songs, have the recordings reproduced and distributed to the public.

Writing your songs and having them performed by an artist is not the end of your work. You have to look into possible consequences and scenario when your songs go public.

What many songwriters fear

- Fear of having their songs stolen. Stealing songs happen but is less common than the fear it induces.

- Stealing ideas is a more concrete fear. Ideas and titles are not copyrighted, therefore, there is a greater possibility that another writer might borrow an idea or a title and use it to come up with a new song.

The notion of an idea being stolen in music has been refuted by many songwriters. A storyteller can choose from many basic plots out of a single idea and after, the storyteller deals with variations. The idea is not the crux of the song but how the writer develops the idea into a song. What makes a song special is the use of language, characterization, and imagery in the song story.

Copyright

The copyright law protects the original songs from the time they are in a tangible medium of expression. Being fixed in a medium of expression means, the creation is on paper or phone record, including tape, vinyl, compact disc, or digital audio file.

If you sing your song or have a performer sing it for you before an audience, your creation is not protected. It has to be written or recorded. It is best for you to have a copyright of your songs and have the symbol visible, placed at the bottom of the first page if it is written, including the year it was written and your name. If your song is recorded on a CD or tape, have the copyright symbol on its page.

Having a copyright means you are the only person who has the right to make copies of your song. But, having a copyright is not enough assurance that your creations are protected. There may be individuals who might dispute ownership of your song. It is, therefore, best to have your songs registered with the copyright agency of your government even before performing it in public.

What is copyright registration?

A copyright registration is not a requirement, nor is it a condition for copyright protection. It is a legal formality that establishes a public record of the basic information of a particular copyright. There are, however, advantages the government gives to encourage copyright owners to register, to wit:

1. Registration establishes a public record of the copyright claim.

2. It is necessary evidence in cases where infringement suit is to be filed in court.

3. Registration establishes evidence which can be used in court that the copyright and the facts contained are valid, provided the registration is made within five years of publication.

4. You can claim statutory damages and attorney's fees in court actions, provided registration is done within 3 months after the work's publication. Beyond the 3 months, the owner of the copyright can only get the profits and actual damages.

What you need to know about copyrights and infringement

Copyright limitation. Song titles and ideas are not protected by copyright. If you hear a song that uses a title of your song as its own, it is not an infringement.

Public Domain. A song is in the public domain if it was written before there were copyright laws, the composer of a song is not known, and when the copyright term has expired. Usually, a copyright expires within 50 or 75 years. Lastly, a work posted on the internet does not necessarily mean it is now a public domain. Neither does downloading a work constitute fair use.

The "doctrine of fair use". Works of writers can be used for certain purposes and not be considered as infringement. These uses include criticism, like when part of a lyric is reproduced for a record review. Another is using a small part of the work as basis in editorial comments or as part of a related news story.

Works can also be used in scholarship or in research, like when it is used for writing term papers or thesis, and in teaching.

You would know what constitutes infringement through the following guidelines:

- Determine the purpose of its use. Is it for nonprofit educational purposes, or is it for commercial purposes?

- What is the nature of the copyright work?

- What is the amount and how substantial is the part used in relation to the whole work?

- What is the effect of the use on the value of, or on the potential market for the copyrighted work?

A Guide To Finding A Good Publisher

For a songwriter, a publisher is like a record label. A good one can advance your career, while a bad one can stand in the way of your progress. You need to consider many factors in choosing the right publisher for our works.

In deciding on a publisher, ask yourself these questions:

1. What is the style of the company?

Publishing companies do the same basic things – licensing artists' works and collecting fees – but they do these things in different ways.

Some music publishers work closely with their songwriters. These companies have a creative team who gets involved with the songwriter and help them develop their work. They give feedback on compositions, offer workshops and seminars to songwriters in their list, or pair up songwriters they see can collaborate well with each other. These publishers are aggressive in generating opportunities for their songwriters and their craft.

On the opposite end, there are publishing companies who view their songwriters as figures in their balance sheet. They expect their songwriters to sign with their companies and excel in what they do. But, they are not involved in the creative process. What they do is to check out works, project potential earnings of a song, and "buy-in" for the share.

If you are a songwriter who wants to sign with a publisher, know how the company operates. Remember that it is to your great advantage to have a publishing company offers support and active in promoting your work.

2. How big is the publishing company?

There are risks for upcoming songwriters to sign with large companies. Ask yourself, how much of a priority are you to a large publishing company? Before you sign with a large company, make sure you have someone in the company who is interested and enthusiastic about your work. Have someone who is responsive to your concerns and questions.

3. Is the publishing company an independent or a major company?

It is often easier for a professional manager to negotiate with producers and artists if they work for a major company. Another advantage with a major company is having the cash flow to invest in development deals.

The debate whether it is better to sign with major or independent publishers has been going on for long. Many would say a songwriter will not get much attention with a major company. But, the amount of attention a songwriter gets from a major company depends on the ratio of professional staff to songwriters.

On the other hand, a small company may have so much to do that they don't have the time to spend working with you on your song. Also, there are small companies who are aggressive publishers, have contacts, and the experience to deal with the right people.

Find out which publisher is the best fit for you? Is it an independent publisher, or a major company with a label?

4. Do you need a publisher?

This question is not easy to answer. Publishing companies are complex and the process of licensing and royalty management consumes much time. A songwriter may find these activities as obstacles in publishing their works. But, ask yourself: Do you have enough knowledge to act as your own publisher. If the answer is yes, ask yourself if you have the time to make publishing your own songs work?

Publishing Your Songs

Publishing is defined in the copyright law in a broad way. **Publication** as used in songwriting business is "the reproduction of a song in the form of any kind of products, printed or recorded, and the offering of those products for sale to the public."

Publishing in practical music, however, is so much more complicated than any legal definition or theory can mean. Music publishing did start with the making and sale of sheet music for piano players. Through technological, social, and economic changes the sale of music sheet is now a small part of music publishing.

Today, the music business centers around films and records, and songwriters play song demos for managers, recording artists, record producers, record companies, and film music supervisors.

With the role publishers plays in the music business, it is important that you know what they do, even if you want to publish music yourself.

The Role Of The Publisher

The concept of publishing comes in different levels and activities. The best publisher demands tenacity, creativity, imagination, and a good business sense. And, a good publisher is not afraid of making mistakes and to face rejection of songs that he believes in. Further, a publisher should also know how the music industry operates and be familiar with the songs of different recording artists – both new and old.

If you are looking for a publisher or want to become your own publisher, then knowing what services to expect from a professional publisher and the qualities possessed is to your benefit.

The four categories of a publisher's activities

Creative – This category includes: meeting new writers, screening new songs, going to recording studios meet budding and established artists, going to night clubs to listen to old and new songs, critiquing works, working with staff and promising independent writers, producing demos, reviewing songs that are in the catalogue, suggesting collaboration or initiating work between staff writers, lyricists, producers, and artists.

Promotional – This category covers contacting agents, managers, producers to know what songs their artists need; reading film, music, advertising trade magazines, tip sheets and periodicals to find projects that need materials; demo mailing; making casting meetings with writers and professional staffers to know which song materials are appropriate for a particular project; keeping files on producers, making tabs on songs they like of don't like, including the songs producers keep on hold; making calls to recording studios, radio stations, and managers to work on promotional ideas.

Business activities – hire personnel; formulate company policies; initiate and sustain contacts with foreign sub-publishers; negotiate contact with writers, music print publishers, artists, producers, managers, TV or film production companies; make decisions on songs for "hold"; negotiate/grant licenses to users.

Administrative duties – These include filing of copyright forms; collecting from record companies; filing notices to agencies that collect mechanical royalties; keeping a general accounting system, tax accounting, and financial planning; computing and paying royalties to writers.

Being Your Own Publisher

To be your own publisher or having a publishing company of your own could mean a great deal for you. The publisher's royalty share represents a substantial amount of money.

There may have been situations where you thought of publishing your works yourself without getting deep into the business. Or, there may have been a few times when you published your songs yourself.

There are other reasons you may want to self-publish, such as:

1. You are a good songwriter and the songs you create are coverable and other artists find merit in recording your songs. You know producers interested in your songs, which means, you have the opportunity to fulfill one of the functions of the publisher.

2. You have the skill to sell yourself. You are an aggressive self-starter and have the potential to be both businessman and creator.

3. You possess a casting sense that enables you to find the right artist for the right song, and at the right time.

4. You are a recording artist who records your own songs. You, therefore, are already doing part of a publisher's job.

5. You have written songs that were successful commercially. Therefore, it is easy for you to get through these doors.

6. Your style of songs is unique that it is unlikely to find artists who will record your songs.

Guide To Starting Your Own Publishing Company

If you think that having your own publishing company is the best course of action, follow this procedure:

1. <u>Choose your company name</u>. Choose the name carefully as you would not want your company name to be similar to another publishing

company. Having a similar name with another company will confuse people. And, it would be unfortunate for your royalties to be sent to another company.

2. <u>Clear your company name</u>. Remember to clear your chosen name with BMI, SESAC, or ASCAP. These organizations are performing rights organizations which can process your application to be a publisher. This is to your advantage, especially if:

    - Records of your works are being released
    - A film is being released which contains your song
    - A television program broadcasts using your work
    - A radio program broadcasts your songs

If you are publishing your own songs, you need only to belong to one performing rights organization. But, if you plan to publish works of other writers who belong to another performing rights organization, you need to establish a publishing company and affiliate it to the one representing your artists.

3. <u>Submit 5 potential names for your company</u>. Be creative in choosing the names for your company. Remember that names that are identical or similar to an existing company will be rejected.

4. <u>Complete the required paper works</u>. You will be required to complete the paper works after your company name is cleared and the affiliation process is accepted. You may inquire from your state for the requirements. You may also be required to file a fictitious name or a "doing-business-as", depending on the state where you belong.

5. <u>Open a bank account</u>. Open a bank account with the name you chose for you publishing company. You need a bank account for cashing checks drafted to your publishing company. For example, cashing mechanical royalty checks and performance checks.

6. <u>Copyright your songs</u>. Have all songs you want included in your company copyrighted. If you happen to have unpublished songs copyrighted, register them again under published works. Having them registered as published works is necessary when the time comes you want to sell your catalog. When you do, the songs in the

catalog need to be proven that they really are your songs.

7. <u>Consult an attorney or an accountant</u>. You need both professional services for legal matters, obtaining business license, a state or federal employer identification number, withhold tax, and report wages. Regulations may vary from different states.

8. <u>Time to organize yourself</u> and keep track of shopping for songs.

Conclusion

Nothing is too difficult and complex for one who has the passion for writing music. If you are determined to put something as abstract as music into print or audio, the content of this book can help make your journey to songwriting easier and more interesting.

Gaining some insight on the elusive nature of music and the processes involved in understanding music hopefully paves the way for understanding it and making it less mysterious. We presented and explained what creativity is to show that it is in our power to be creative, and not something only a few possess.

The technicalities involved in creating songs are explained to give you the skills you need to create songs that appeal to the public and would last long in their memories.

But your journey to becoming a professional songwriter does not end with reading the book. It takes patience and practice to have the art and the craft become second skin to you. Your love of writing songs may continue and motivate you to have your works published yourself.

Believe in yourself and you can go beyond your expectations.

I'd like to thank you and congratulate you for transiting my lines from start to finish.

I hope this book was able to help you pursue your passion of writing songs and become a professional songwriter.

The next step is to start writing now. Get those musical ideas and express them into lyrics and music.

I wish you the best of luck!

Tommy Swindali

Thanks for Reading!

What did you think of, **Music Elements: Music Theory, Songwriting, Lyrics & Creativity Explained**

I know you could have picked any number of books to read, but you picked this book and for that I am extremely grateful.

I hope that it added at value and quality to your everyday life. If so, it would be really nice if you could share this book with your friends and family by posting to Facebook and Twitter.

If you enjoyed this book and found some benefit in reading this, I'd like to hear from you and hope that you could take some time to post a review. Your feedback and support will help this author to greatly improve his writing craft for future projects and make this book even better.

I want you, the reader, to know that your review is very important and so, if you'd like to leave a review, all you have to do is click here and away you go. I wish you all the best in your future success!

Also check out my other books:

In The Mix: Discover The Secrets to Becoming a Successful DJ

Music Production: Everything You Need To Know About Producing Music and Songwriting

Music Production: How to Produce Music, The Easy to Read Guide for Music Producers Introduction

Songwriting: Apply Proven Methods, Ideas and Exercises to Kickstart or Upgrade Your Songwriting

Thank you and good luck!

Claim This Now

Music Business Skills for Musicians:

If you're in the music business, read on. Today you need to view yourself through the new rules of the music industry.

Those who play by them will succeed.

Gone are the old days where you would hope to get signed and then become a star (i.e., everything would be done for you).

Do you wonder why other artists are getting breaks and you are not?

MUSIC BUSINESS SKILLS FOR MUSICIANS

Make Money from Music, Discover The Music Industry and Explode Your Music Career!

TOMMY SWINDALI

Are You Ready To Start Earning REAL INCOME With Your Music?

https://www.subscribepage.com/musicbiz

Made in the USA
San Bernardino, CA
16 April 2020